Evil Agenda

EVIL AGENDA

The Ultimate Conspiracy

WAYNE BRADLEY

And have no fellowship with the unfruitful works of darkness, but rather expose them. (Eph. 5:11)

All Bible citations are from the New King James Version.

ISBN-13: 9780692615584
ISBN-10: 069261558X
WB Publishing, LLC

Table of Contents

Making Sense out of the Senseless

> But know this, that in the last days perilous times will come: For men will be lovers of themselves, lovers of money, boasters, proud, blasphemers, disobedient to parents, unthankful, unholy, unloving, unforgiving, slanderers, without self-control, brutal, despisers of good, traitors, headstrong, haughty, lovers of pleasure rather than lovers of God, having a form of godliness but denying its power. And from such people turn away! (2 Tim. 3:1–5)

We are currently living in a time where our culture is evolving in ways that make no sense whatsoever. Everything seems to be running backward. Good is bad and bad is good. Right is wrong and wrong is right. The truth is relative, and there are no moral absolutes. Men can be women, and women can be men (or both in some cases). Our culture appears to be more concerned about the killing of a lion than they are about the news of Planned Parenthood employees selling baby parts. Our government keeps Christian refugees from Syria and Afghanistan in captivity while releasing illegal aliens that are known felons. They deport Christian refugees while Muslim refugees are granted asylum without vetting. That same government negotiates a trade to release five Taliban terrorist commanders for one US Army deserter. Our laws require children to get permission from their parents to take aspirin, but no such permission is required for a taxpayer-funded abortion. And the most absurd notion of all: our politicians tell us that they need to spend *more* money to get out of our debt crisis.

It is as if our culture and our economy are on a sinking ship full of holes and our leaders tell us that we need to drill holes in the hull to let the water out. Out of our ignorance and/or apathy, we continue to go down this (wrong) path despite these leaders' long track record of failure. Why do we allow this lunacy to continue right before our eyes and always blame someone else? It makes no sense.

On the other hand, when you examine the evidence within the right context, it actually makes perfect sense. In the coming pages, we will examine the current trends in our culture as we make sense out of the senseless. We will examine a series of observations from everyday life that will provide evidence from a very unique perspective to answer the question as to whether or not God exists. While there are already numerous books out there that highlight the fingerprints of God, this text takes a back-door approach. Rather than listing the countless examples of miracles, testimonies, and biblical and historical documentation, we will examine the evidence of God from a perspective of the existence and proliferation of evil. Rather than trying to prove that God exists, why not start with the reverse approach and point out the overwhelming evidence of the evil one and his influence? Indeed, if there is an evil one, Satan, wouldn't there also be God? If you believe in God, then it should be easy to conclude that Satan also exists. But on the other hand, the reverse is probably also true. If you do not believe in God, then you probably do not believe in Satan either and can even dismiss the existence of evil.

> Little children, it is the last hour; and as you have heard that the Antichrist is coming, even now many antichrists have come, by which we know that it is the last hour. (1 John 2:18)

Most people would agree that evil represents something that is bad, but you may have trouble getting a strict definition because of moral relativism. As a matter of fact, an atheist may not believe in "evil" at all. Merriam-Webster.

com defines *evil* as "morally reprehensible: sinful, wicked," and at first glance, this seems like an obvious and clear definition. But how do you define *moral, sinful,* or *wicked*? Merriam-Webster.com's definition of *sin* includes "an offense against religious or moral law." Merriam-Webster.com defines *wicked* as "morally very bad." You can see this presents a problem for people who do not have religious beliefs, since *sinful, wicked,* and *morally bad* may not have meaning in their belief systems. A worldly person may have a much more liberal view than a Christian, therefore, we will also include a much more definitive position as we present and examine the evidence. Specifically, let's take a look at the proliferation of evil and anti-Christian sentiment in our time and how it has infiltrated every aspect of our culture. The attacks on Christians and traditional Christian values have never been more pronounced, are increasing, and frankly, do not make any sense.

> We hold these truths to be self-evident, that all men are created equal, that they are endowed by their Creator with certain unalienable Rights, that among these are Life, Liberty and the pursuit of Happiness.
>
> —The Declaration of Independence

Because politics can be such an emotionally charged subject and can easily turn people off, it would be preferable to avoid these discussions. However, because revisionists are attempting to rewrite history, it is worth pointing out the fact that this country was clearly founded on a strong belief in God as well as personal freedom. If you believe this statement makes this book partisan and you are ready to throw it in the trash, just hang on, because there is a chapter later in the book written just for you.

> If you indeed obey the Lord your God and are careful to observe all his commandments I am giving you today, the Lord your God will elevate you above all the nations of the earth. All these blessings will come to you in abundance if you obey the Lord your God. (Deut. 28:1–2)

There is no question that the United States has prospered immensely during the last 240-plus years because of its principle of putting God first. We will examine the current state of the country as political correctness continues to remove God and religious expression and highlight the resultant effect this is having on the state of our country.

As we proceed, it is important that the reader understands what it means to be a Christian, so we need to touch on some basics before we can move forward. However, be assured that the analysis in this book is intended to be very scientific in nature, utilizing accepted scientific and legal principles. To begin, here are a select few scriptures to provide some insight on what it means to be a Christian.

> For God so loved the world that He gave His only begotten Son, that whoever believes in Him should not perish but have everlasting life. (John 3:16)

> For all have sinned and fall short of the glory of God. (Rom. 3:23)

> But the fruit of the Spirit is love, joy, peace, longsuffering, kindness, goodness, faithfulness, gentleness, self-control. Against such there is no law. (Gal. 5:22–23)

The Bible teaches us that nobody is without sin but that God loved us so much that He sent His Son, Jesus, to die on the cross in full payment for those sins so that we can have a relationship with Him. Basically, true Christians are those who accept Jesus as their Lord and Savior and believe this is the *only* path to God and heaven. While Christians admit we are sinners, it is our desire to become more Christlike as we progress in our walk with the Lord. We expect to reap the fruits of the Spirit as we mature. True Christians live their lives for Christ, nurturing those fruits that all people should believe is a good thing, regardless of their belief or lack of belief in the God of the universe. So, if the essence of Christianity is good, why is there so much anti-Christian sentiment, and why is it increasing so dramatically? Why is there such an all-out assault on Christianity, the Bible, and God? Some of the things we'll examine are everyday occurrences, and others you won't believe are really happening around the world, much less here in America. This text is very simply an attempt to expose evil in its many forms as we make sense of the senseless. In essence, we will be conducting a scientific experiment to prove the existence of God by asking the question: If there is a Satan, what would he do any differently?

> The fear of the Lord is the beginning of knowledge, but fools despise wisdom and instruction. (Prov. 1:7)

Science is a systematic enterprise that builds and organizes knowledge in the form of testable explanations and predictions about the universe. The word *science* comes from the Latin word *scientia*, which means knowledge. To have and seek knowledge is a good thing, and more knowledge is better than less knowledge. (As a sidenote for the scientists out there, it should be noted that Proverbs 1:7 can be interpreted as "The fear of the Lord is the beginning of science…") So let's examine what it means to analyze something scientifically and what it takes to develop a proof. Keep in mind this is exactly how science develops and tests the information that is written in countless science books and is taught in schools and universities around the globe. The steps include the following:

- Ask a question.
- Develop a hypothesis.
- Test your hypothesis.
- Analyze data.
- Draw a conclusion.
- Repeat as often as necessary.

In the legal and scientific world, there are several standards for burden of proof, including but not necessarily limited to:

- credible evidence,
- preponderance of the evidence,
- clear and convincing evidence, and
- beyond a reasonable doubt.

Beyond a reasonable doubt is defined on www.freedictionary.com as:[1]

> The standard that must be met by the prosecution's evidence in a criminal prosecution: that no other logical explanation can be derived from the facts except that the defendant committed the crime, thereby overcoming the presumption that a person is innocent until proven guilty...
>
> The term connotes that evidence establishes a particular point to a moral certainty and that it is beyond dispute that any reasonable alternative is possible. It does not mean that no doubt exists as to the accused's guilt, but only that no Reasonable Doubt is possible from the evidence presented.

Think about all you have learned in school that you currently accept as fact and the level of proof that has been obtained. How many programs have you watched on TV explaining our natural history that you easily accepted as scientific fact and did not question? For example, science suggests that the earth is billions of years old, yet there is absolutely no way to prove it. Nonetheless, it is widely accepted as fact because science cannot provide any other explanation in worldly terms. Did you know the earth is aging at the rate of millions of years per day? Science keeps revising the estimate of the earth's age because scientists cannot fit certain explanations in the current model. When they come to a question they cannot answer, they simply tack on another couple of million years to explain it.

> But there were also false prophets among the people, even as there will be false teachers among you, who will secretly bring in

> destructive heresies, even denying the Lord who bought them, and bring on themselves swift destruction. And many will follow their destructive ways, because of whom the way of truth will be blasphemed. (2 Pet. 2:1–2)

Science also tries to teach us that all life, including humans, evolved from lower forms of life through natural selection. If this is true, wouldn't you believe that changing from one species (kind) to another would take a really, *really* long time? Wouldn't you think there would be ample evidence in the fossil record documenting interspecies evolution? Darwin's own theories state that life does not jump. If indeed this was the natural order of the world, wouldn't there be evidence to support that this process is continuing? Did the world finally reach equilibrium, and evolution just decided to stop?

> Knowing this first: that scoffers will come in the last days, walking according to their own lusts, and saying, "Where is the promise of His coming? For since the fathers fell asleep, all things continue as they were from the beginning of creation." For this they willfully forget: that by the word of God the heavens were of old, and the earth standing out of water and in the water, by which the world that then existed perished, being flooded with water. (2 Pet. 3:3–6)

Consider this equation: There is an Olympic-size swimming pool that we want to fill using a leaking hose that deposits one drop of water every second. In order to calculate the time required to fill the pool, we would determine the average volume of water per drop and divide it into the volume of the pool, taking into consideration any evaporation that may take place. Under controlled circumstances, your calculation may indicate that it would take thousands of years to fill. However, this calculation is based on existing conditions as we know them today. Changes in climate, temperature, and humidity (as well as rainfall) can affect the results by a huge margin. Unfortunately, many scientists ignore these possible variations to make their conclusions. This is called uniformitarianism. Merriam-Webster.com states that *uniformitarianism* is a "doctrine in geology that physical, chemical, and biologic processes now at work on and within the Earth have operated with general uniformity (in the same manner and with essentially the same intensity) through immensely long periods of time and are sufficient to account for all geologic change." While this is a valid assumption in the absence of information to the contrary, you cannot ignore that it is, in fact, an assumption.

To help illustrate this point, let's examine carbon dating for a moment. We are taught that science can utilize carbon dating to estimate the age of ancient artifacts. Did you know that the procedure is based on at least three assumptions that cannot be proven? They include:

1. atmospheric conditions have always been constant,
2. the rate of decay in C12/C14 is constant, and
3. the original amount of C12/C14 is known.

Did you know that countless blind studies have been conducted that prove how inaccurate carbon dating really is? Did you know that samples from the same specimen have yielded results that indicate thousands of years' difference in age? Two samples from the exact same artifact produce age estimates of thousands of years apart, yet this is a scientifically accepted method.

> The works of the Lord are great, Studied by all who have pleasure in them. (Ps. 111:2)

> It is the glory of God to conceal a matter, but the glory of kings is to search out a matter. (Prov. 25:2)

Be assured this is not an attempt to disparage science or scientists in any way. As a matter of fact, we do benefit from science, and we need to be able to explain things in terms people can understand. The problem comes when science treats this information as fact when much of it is actually only theory that may never be proven. Indeed, if you believe in everything the world teaches us about natural history without question, then you have an amazing faith in something you cannot see, touch, hear, smell, or taste, and that has never been observed or recreated in science. As much as the science establishment may try to deny it, this is a fact.

With this in mind, if we were going to try to prove that God (or Satan) exists, what level of proof would be required for most people? What would it take to convince you? Unfortunately, there are many that would not believe in God even if He appeared right in front of them. There are countless stories in the Bible of how God revealed himself (e.g., Garden of Eden, Exodus, miracles of Jesus, and so on), yet people still turned away after experiencing Him firsthand. Nonetheless, in the coming pages evidence will be presented in a clear and systematic manner in an attempt to reach the highest standard of proof possible. Our true question is simply: Does God exist? Our hypothesis is as follows: If the God of the Bible exists, then the existence of Satan is also real. Since there is no way to see God within our earthly confines, we seek evidence of the existence of Satan. Since Satan is the great deceiver, then we may not be able to see him either, or at least we may not know it at the time. Therefore, we must further examine what we know about Satan and develop experiments to test for his existence and the existence of his works.

†††

Let's begin from a scientific perspective with the theory that Satan does exist. We are now challenged with trying to develop an experiment to test for the existence of evil. Think of the problem from a modern viewpoint. If you were trying to make a historically accurate movie about the conflict between God and Satan, what would that relationship look like?

> Well, there are all manner of lesser imps and demons, Pete, but the great Satan himself is red and scaly with a bifurcated tail, and he carries a hay fork.
>
> —Ulysses Everett McGill in *O Brother, Where Art Thou?*[2]

First, we have the Bible, which Christians believe to be the Word of God. The Bible also contains numerous references to Satan and the evil one, whom we'll simply refer to as Satan. Unfortunately, those references are often referred to with symbolism, so we may have to use our imaginations. As a matter of fact, most of our preconceived notions of Satan were born in Hollywood and injected into our brains via the television and the silver screen.

For humor's sake, let's imagine Satan from an authoritative perspective in today's terms. Specifically, Satan is the chairman of the board, and his minions are his directors. The sole purpose of his organization is to try to undermine the God of the Bible and keep us from His Will for our lives. In order to be effective, he needs to understand the audience and play to their vulnerabilities, and he will utilize any available resource necessary to accomplish his objectives. It may actually be a useful and revealing exercise to be divided into groups in competition to come up with the most effective ideas for undermining God and advancing Satan's agenda. Participants would know their own weaknesses and possibly the weaknesses of their friends and relatives. It is likely they could come up with some brilliant ideas that may be useful in helping them be prepared for Satan's influence. If you knew someone was out to destroy you and control your life, wouldn't you be better prepared to defend yourself if you could anticipate some of the problems and strategies? Wouldn't it help to have your opponent's playbook? (This would make an excellent TV series.)

To help demonstrate this concept, think about the art of advertising. There are college curriculums available that help prepare a student to make a career in advertising. Billions of dollars are spent each year on countless strategies to convince consumers to buy specific products. This is not meant to suggest that advertising is not an honorable profession; rather, it suggests that there are countless researched strategies to make advertising more effective in influencing people's beliefs and actions.

If the greatest deceiver in the world was the chairman of the board of an agency that promoted an anti-Christian agenda to try to divert people from doing God's Will for their lives, what would those strategies look like? If the greatest advertising minds in the world came together to further this effort, can you imagine the creative ideas they would develop to further this agenda? Just think about how clever the great deceiver is. In the coming chapters, we will expose evidence for just a few of these strategies, and with a little imagination, perhaps we can predict some possible future ones.

So what do we expect from Satan? What does he look like? What does he want? What is his agenda? Well, if you think about it, isn't the answer actually pretty straightforward? Satan represents the antithesis of God. God is good; Satan is evil. God loves us; Satan despises us and God. God wants us to care for one another; Satan wants pain and suffering. God wants order; Satan wants anarchy. God wants us to have a relationship with Him; Satan wants to prevent and/or destroy that relationship. God is love; Satan is hate. God represents Truth; Satan represents lies and deceit. God wants to be Lord of our lives; Satan wants to control our lives. With this in mind, wouldn't you expect Satan and his accomplices to try to achieve power and influence over our lives in every way possible? Wouldn't you expect him to lie about his methods and motives to achieve his agenda?

The next chapter provides a snapshot from a biblical perspective on who and what Satan is, what we might expect from his character, and how to recognize his works and influence. After that, the next step in our experiment will be to test our hypothesis by analyzing the data with the hopes of reaching a conclusion. Because the term *evil* may be relative to your belief system and because other religions also refer to Satan, we need to be more specific in our analysis and also look for the prevalence and proliferation of anti-Christian views and attitudes.

Satan's Character

> And have no fellowship with the unfruitful works of darkness, but rather expose them. (Eph. 5:11)

In order to test for the presence of Satan, the devil, or evil, we need an accurate description of his character and his works. Because we expect Satan to hide his true nature, we need to develop an experiment to detect his influence. We need to put aside the images and characterizations that Hollywood has portrayed and take a look at the description of Satan and evil from the single most authoritative source, the Bible. The following are select verses:

> Then the serpent said to the woman, "You will not surely die. For God knows that in the day you eat of it your eyes will be opened, and you will be like God, knowing good and evil." (Gen. 3:4–5)

In the Garden of Eden, Satan personally attacked the authority of our Sovereign God and tried to convince Eve that God is not who He says He is. Satan used lies and deceit to convince Adam and Eve to disobey God's Will for their lives. Our expectation is that Satan will try to attack the sovereignty of God to subvert His Will for our lives.

> Then Jesus was led up by the Spirit into the wilderness to be tempted by the devil. (Matt. 4:1)

> And he said to Him, "All these things I will give You if You will fall down and worship me." Then Jesus said to him, "Away with you, Satan! For it is written, 'You shall worship the Lord your God, and Him only you shall serve.'" (Matt. 4:9–10)

Just as he attempted to lure Jesus away from His Father, Satan will try to tempt us away from God with lies and deceit and promises of worldly things, or at the very least, he will try to distract us.

> Therefore hear the parable of the sower: When anyone hears the word of the kingdom, and does not understand it, then the wicked one comes and snatches away what was sown in his heart. This is he who received seed by the wayside. (Matt. 13:18–19)

> And these are the ones by the wayside where the word is sown. When they hear, Satan comes immediately and takes away the word that was sown in their hearts. (Mark 4:15)

Satan will try to fill our minds with confusion to keep us from understanding and believing in the Word, including trying to convince us there is no God and/or trying to convince us the gospel is useless. Our expectation is that Satan will harden the hearts of some to keep them from receiving the gospel.

> [But] while men slept, his enemy came and sowed tares among the wheat and went his way. (Matt. 13:25)

The actual, literal interpretation is that the enemy came and sowed "darnel," which is a poisonous weed that *looks* like wheat. In other words, there will be Christian impersonators who will try to corrupt God's plan and further Satan's agenda. Our expectation is that Satan will try to corrupt the church from within.

> And Jesus came and spoke to them, saying, "All authority has been given to Me in heaven and on earth. Go therefore and make disciples

> of all the nations, baptizing them in the name of the Father and of the Son and of the Holy Spirit, teaching them to observe all things that I have commanded you; and lo, I am with you always, even to the end of the age." Amen. (Matt. 28:18–20)

> And He said to them, "Go into all the world and preach the gospel to every creature." (Mark 16:15)

The Bible explicitly commands Christians to share the gospel with the entire world, which is commonly referred to as the Great Commission. Because Satan cannot change the minds of all believers, his goal is to try to prevent new converts, thereby eliminating Christianity through attrition. Our expectation is that Satan and his accomplices will use any means possible to prevent Christians from sharing the gospel.

> But when He had turned around and looked at His disciples, He rebuked Peter, saying, "Get behind Me, Satan! For you are not mindful of the things of God, but the things of men." (Mark 8:33)

Keep in mind that what is best for God is not necessarily what we think is best. Our expectation is that Satan will try to convince us that God's Will for our lives is not the best path.

> And the Lord said, "Simon, Simon! Indeed, Satan has asked for you, that he may sift you as wheat. But I have prayed for you, that your faith should not fail; and when you have returned to Me, strengthen your brethren." But he said to Him, "Lord, I am ready to go with You, both to prison and to death." (Luke 22:31–33)

Satan wants to snatch as many people away from God as he can. Again, our expectation is that Satan will be relentless in corrupting our lives.

> But Peter said, "Ananias, why has Satan filled your heart to lie to the Holy Spirit and keep back for yourself part of the proceeds from

> the sale of the land? Before it was sold, did it not belong to you? And when it was sold, was the money not at your disposal? How have you thought up this deed in your heart? You have not lied to people but to God!" (Acts 5:3–4)

Our expectation is that Satan will try to convince us that we can lie in our hearts and God will not know.

> But I fear, lest somehow, as the serpent deceived Eve by his craftiness, so your minds may be corrupted from the simplicity that is in Christ. For if he who comes preaches another Jesus whom we have not preached, or if you receive a different spirit which you have not received, or a different gospel which you have not accepted—you may well put up with it! (2 Cor. 11:3–4)

Mormonism[3] is a good example of this concept, where the adherents proclaim a *different* Jesus Christ. Joseph Smith, the founder of Mormonism, was born in the early nineteenth century and taught that all Christianity was an abomination because it had been distorted over time. Joseph Smith is attributed with interpreting the Book of Mormon, another testament of Jesus Christ. Our expectation is that Satan will use any means possible to divert us from the one True God and the only path to Him, the True Jesus Christ.

> For such people are false apostles, deceitful workers, disguising themselves as apostles of Christ. And no wonder, for even Satan disguises himself as an angel of light. Therefore it is not surprising his servants also disguise themselves as servants of righteousness, whose end will correspond to their actions. (2 Cor. 11:13–15)

There have been and will continue to be examples of false prophets and false Christian leaders. A couple of the more terrifying examples from recent history include David Koresh and Jim Jones. Our expectation is that Satan's accomplices will provide false interpretations of the Word to try to lead us away from God.

> Therefore we wanted to come to you—even I, Paul, time and again—but Satan hindered us. (1 Thess. 2:18)

Our expectation is that Satan will use any means possible to keep us from seeking God and achieving His Will for our lives.

> For we do not wrestle against flesh and blood, but against principalities, against powers, against the rulers of the darkness of this age, against spiritual hosts of wickedness in the heavenly places. (Eph. 6:12)

This highlights one of the most important concepts of this book. Our struggle against evil is not confined to worldly matters within our control; it is against the forces of evil and the ruler of darkness. We cannot defeat evil without God's help, and by not accepting God, we are by default accepting evil.

> Do not deprive one another except with consent for a time, that you may give yourselves to fasting and prayer; and come together again so that Satan does not tempt you because of your lack of self-control. (1 Cor. 7:5)

Our expectation is that Satan will attempt to lure us away from our walk with God by using sexual temptations contrary to biblical principles.

> He who sins is of the devil, for the devil has sinned from the beginning. For this purpose the Son of God was manifested, that He might destroy the works of the devil. (1 John 3:8)

At every opportunity, Satan will try to tempt us with sin, claiming pride, lust, greed, anger, slothfulness, envy, and gluttony lead to self-fulfillment.

> In this the children of God and the children of the devil are manifest: Whoever does not practice righteousness is not of God, nor is he who does not love his brother. (1 John 3:10)

If you are not with God, you are against God. There are many that are unintentionally doing Satan's will by not following God's Will for their lives. Although unintentional, their actions may still be supportive of Satan's agenda.

> The coming of the lawless one is according to the working of Satan, with all power, signs, and lying wonders, and with all unrighteous deception among those who perish, because they did not receive the love of the truth, that they might be saved. (2 Thess. 2:9–10)

This is a prophecy regarding end-times; however, keep this in mind, as the hour is late. Our expectation is that Satan will try to use all kinds of wonders to keep us from discovering God.

> But even if our gospel is veiled, it is veiled to those who are perishing, whose minds the god of this age has blinded, who do not believe, lest the light of the gospel of the glory of Christ, who is the image of God, should shine on them. (2 Cor. 4:3–4)

Our expectation is that Satan will try to convince us there is no God.

> Do not fear any of those things which you are about to suffer. Indeed, the devil is about to throw some of you into prison, that you may be tested, and you will have tribulation ten days. Be faithful until death, and I will give you the crown of life. (Rev. 2:10)

This highlights another important point of this book. Satan will be seeking to persecute Christians in order to corrupt God's Will for our lives.

As previously stated, Satan represents the antithesis of God, and our expectation is that Satan will promote and encourage any activity that will keep us from God's Will for our lives. We expect him to use any means possible to keep us from sharing our faith with others, just as he will do anything to keep people from receiving it. Further, Satan will sow evil (darnel) among the righteous in order to try to corrupt religious institutions from within. Satan will try to convince us there is no God, and where he falls short, he will try to convince us that we do not need God or that religion is in itself evil. Our expectation also includes an emphasis on hostility toward and persecution of Christians (anti-Christ) aimed specifically at impeding the Great Commission.

We have our question: Does God exist? We have developed a hypothesis: If the God of the Bible exists, then Satan (and evil) also exists. Now let's move forward with our scientific methodology and test our hypothesis. As we move forward, please have an open mind and be thinking proactively about the possibilities.

Satan's Number-One Strategy

> Also I say to you, whoever confesses Me before men, him the Son of Man also will confess before the angels of God. But he who denies Me before men will be denied before the angels of God. (Luke 12:8–9)

If there is a great Satan and his nature and purpose are clearly forewarned in the Bible, how could he function effectively with his agenda and purpose so clearly exposed? What strategy could he use to overcome this portrait of his true self? The first and most obvious strategy is convincing people there is no God and hence no Satan. If someone truly believes Satan is not real, then he can operate in complete stealth under the premise that you don't need to fear something that does not exist.

Imagine, if you can, an organization based on a common shared belief that the tooth fairy or Santa Claus does not exist. Not only is it an organization but a movement. How successful do you think that movement would be at recruiting members? What purpose would it serve? Why would someone be motivated to participate in an organization dedicated to a nonbelief in a mythical character? Merriam-Webster.com defines *atheist* as "one who believes that there is no deity." An Internet search on the term *atheist* resulted in more than forty-five million hits. Why would there be so many websites dedicated to denying the existence of the God of the Bible? Why are there atheist support groups? If you really believe the accounts of the Bible are fairy tales (or myths), why is it necessary to be so hostile toward Christian organizations? Why aren't there similar atheist crusades against Islam, Buddhism, or Hinduism? If you believe atheists deny the existence of any god, well, think again! Most atheist resources are not only dedicated to trying to prove there is no God, but most are downright hostile toward Christianity and even stretch the truth and make ridiculous associations in order to make Christianity look bad. (Perform an Internet search on the term *atheist* and see for yourself the countless examples.)

Why are so much money and so many resources spent on this effort? Are they concerned that Christians are just wasting their time when they could be doing something much more productive? Are they worried about the money Christians spend on helping the needy all around the world? Are they concerned that Christian ministers are hoodwinking their parishioners into voluntarily giving them 10 percent of their income? Are they concerned about Christians' desire to be more Christlike? Do you believe for the slightest moment they will have *any* effect on a true Christian believer? Do you believe for a moment that committed atheists frequent these websites, and if they do, why? Do they need to be reassured that their atheistic beliefs are valid? So, who are they there for? As a matter of fact, there is an article on www.richarddawkins.net that specifically states: "Debating creationists offer[s] their position credibility."[4] The motives are obvious and can only be explained as Satan's attempts to place doubt into vulnerable minds and to provide comfort to those adherents of atheism.

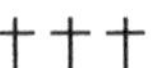

There is a movie called *Expelled: No Intelligence Allowed,*[5] hosted by Ben Stein, that helps expose the atheist assault on religion by the scientific establishment. To help explain the subject of the movie, you need to understand a concept called intelligent design. *Intelligent design* is a term used in science that is a theory to explain things that cannot be explained by Darwin's theory of evolution or other scientific theory. Intelligentdesign.org[6] states that it refers to a "scientific research" program that "seeks evidence of design in nature." They further explain that the "theory of intelligent design holds that certain features of the universe and of living things are best explained by an intelligent cause, not an undirected process such as natural selection." To provide you with some excellent examples of intelligent design, there are some really good videos called *Creatures That Defy Evolution,*[7] which has three volumes. In these documentaries, Dr. Jobe Martin very articulately examines a variety of strange and unique characteristics of different creatures and postulates that there is no logical way they could have evolved naturally.

> The subject of instinct might have been worked into the previous chapters; but I have thought that it would be more convenient to treat the subject separately, especially as so wonderful an instinct as that of the hive-bee making its cells will probably have occurred to many readers, as a difficulty sufficient to overthrow my whole theory.
>
> —Charles Darwin, *On the Origin of Species*,[8] Chapter 7, Instinct

Before atheists get defensive, intelligent design does not necessarily equate to religion or creationism. Essentially, it is a term used to fill the holes in Darwin's theory of evolution, and yes, there are many. Even Darwin himself admitted there are weaknesses in his theory, and chapter 6 of his book *On the Origin of Species*[8] is entitled "Difficulties in the Theory," but that is not the point to be made here. Since *intelligent design* is a scientific term, you would think it would be used by scientists, right? The movie *Expelled: No Intelligence Allowed* documents example after example of well-respected scientists, some of whom had tenure at their respective institutions, who have lost their jobs for so much as mentioning the theory. Because the science establishment is so afraid that intelligent design weakens the theory of evolution, it has been essentially barred from even asking the question.

In the movie, a noted atheist and evolutionist, Richard Dawkins, states that evolution is a fact and "is established as securely as any other fact" they have in science. He goes on to say that most people who don't believe in evolution are "ignorant." He even wrote a book called *The God Delusion*, which he explained as a "full frontal attack on religion"; however, in the movie, Dawkins states that he is an atheist with respect to the "Judeo-Christian God." He did not say there is no god. He did not say that there is no creator. He specifically stated that he is an atheist with respect to the "Judeo-Christian" God. Surely this man of science, a person who deals in facts, knows that Christians only account for less than one-third of the people who associate with religious beliefs worldwide. Why do you suppose he singled out the God of the Bible?

> He who is of God hears God's words; therefore you do not hear, because you are not of God. (John 8:47)

Toward the end of the movie, Ben Stein asked Mr. Dawkins straight out if he believed in any god, and his answer was an emphatic no. But when pressed whether intelligent design could be possible, his answer was "maybe." He basically stated that intelligent design could explain life on Earth but only if other intelligent beings (i.e., aliens) were responsible, but he qualified his answer by stating that the aliens would have "evolved" somewhere else. This so-called man of science postulated that aliens could be responsible for life on Earth, but the aliens would have been created through evolution somewhere else. Where do you think Mr. Dawkins got the evidence to support his emphatic conclusion? Do you get the significance of his statement? Intelligent design isn't worth talking about, but it is acceptable to theorize that aliens could be responsible for life on Earth.

In another clip from the movie, when asked how life began, another scientist suggested that it could have happened on the "backs of crystals," or it was even suggested, again, that it could have started from extraterrestrial origin. *Any* explanation for the beginnings of life is on the table except intelligent design. Why? Because they are afraid it could lead to having to admit that evolution is only a theory.

Note how atheists are arguing that science and religion cannot coexist. Why would discovering and explaining how natural processes work have to be contrary to an all-knowing God? If there is a God and He created all things, wouldn't it follow that He wrote the laws of nature and physics? How does discovering the mysteries of the universe conflict with the existence of God? If God created us in His image, wouldn't it follow that He gave us intelligence and that we would eventually figure out at least some of life's mysteries?

Suppose science was eventually able to prove the existence of God—or if you want to think in worldly terms, suppose life on Earth was deposited by aliens. If scientists are not even allowed to ask the question, how could they ever reach that conclusion? Imagine for a moment that life on Earth did begin from extraterrestrial origins rather than evolution. Based on the evidence presented in the movie *Expelled: No Intelligence Allowed*, it appears that scientists risk their careers by straying from the party line. You discuss intelligent design, you lose your tenure, you lose your funding, and you lose your job. If science is truly about finding answers, why would it be so dangerous just to ask the question? The answer is simple: Satan cannot compete with the Truth, so he tries to obscure it.

These not-so-subtle assaults on God have been occurring for decades with the assistance of the major media. Some past and more contemporary examples include the following:

- On April 8, 1966, *Time* magazine was published with the cover asking the question "Is God Dead?"[9] According to Wikipedia.org, the article cited that science's ability to explain our origins reduced the relevance of needing a God to explain things. The article is one of many seeds planted in the minds of the vulnerable to inject doubt. As a sidenote, the Church of Satan was founded later that same month.
- In 2007, *Nightline* hosted a Face-Off segment entitled "Does God Exist?"[10] where the moderator paired off two atheists, Brian Sapient and Kelly (neither of which is apparently their true name), against two Christians, Kirk Cameron and Ray Comfort. While the audience was reported to be a mix of atheists and Christians and despite the fact that the debate was held in a church, it was obvious there were many more atheists than Christians in the audience, or at least they were certainly more vocal. While the dialogue was somewhat offensive and the majority of the audience stacked against Christianity, Kirk and Ray clearly dominated the debate. Ray Comfort presented

a brilliant example of clear and undisputable proof that a Creator exists. In short, in the same way you cannot have a painting without a painter or a building without a builder, you cannot have a creation without a Creator. On the other hand, Brian Sapient took the opportunity to proudly boast about his anti-Christian website called blasphemychallenge.com.[11] Brian stated that the website's purpose was to "strip the power from religious institutions." While his motives are obvious, he doesn't even have the courage to state the complete truth and admit the site's purpose is to strip the power from *Christian* institutions. This site is predicated around a single verse from guess where? The Bible. If indeed the argument is that there is no God or gods, why exclusively limit your argument to Christianity? Toward the end of the program, the moderator asked Brian and Kelly, "What if you are wrong?" Kelly responded by stating, "I would rather go to hell than go to Heaven and worship a megalomaniacal tyrant." Sadly, Kelly actually had the courage to reveal her true character. Who does this sound like?

- In 2009, ABC News aired a Face-Off segment entitled "Does Satan Exist?"[12] For whom was this topic aired? Christians should already know that Satan does exist, and nonbelievers are convinced that both God and Satan are fictitious characters. This leaves the people who may be on the fence or those who don't already know enough about their own beliefs to know the answer, or people who do not believe in God but want to somehow validate their beliefs. If you take time to watch the video, you will see that the conversations very clearly undermined the principles and teachings of the Bible. The panel even included a person referred to as a bishop (a man of the cloth), who not only suggested that evil was misunderstood, but he even posed the question as to whether God was male or female. Why in the world was this man on this discussion panel representing Christianity (or whatever religion he claimed to be bishop of)? Why host such an event on national TV, other than to place doubt into people's minds?

But please don't misunderstand. God's Word will always triumph over evil. While we can welcome the debate, please notice the way the

> media had stacked the deck in favor of the negative view. Do you honestly believe this panel was the best choice in representing Christian values and beliefs? Wouldn't it make sense to provide biblical scholars on the panel? On the other hand, why did this news story focus solely on Christianity? Christianity is not the only religion that believes in Satan.

In February 2014, there was a debate between Ken Ham and Bill Nye ("the Science Guy") entitled "Creation vs. Evolution."[13] The entire debate was approximately two and a half hours long, so it does require a little bit of a commitment to sit through. Nonetheless, it was interesting and worth watching. While both sides claimed victory, please take the time to see for yourself. While you are watching, please consider this brief analysis. Ken Ham's opening arguments were very compelling in exposing weaknesses in the theory of evolution (please note the title of the debate), and he related those weaknesses to the accounts of the Bible. On the other hand, Bill Nye spent the vast majority of his opening remarks making the case for a very old Earth. In essence, it appeared that his point was that Earth is billions of years old; hence, there couldn't possibly be a god. Again, note the title of the debate. Is this what Bill Nye calls good science? While Bill Nye did provide some arguments for evolution later in the debate, he was completely ineffective in responding to the evidence presented by Ken Ham and, in fact, appeared to avoid the hard questions altogether. Listening to atheist resources argue about having the debate at all was just as interesting as the debate itself. There was one video of a young lady claiming it was a bad idea for Bill Nye to debate Ken Ham because the latter was a more experienced debater than the former, in essence making excuses before the debate ever began. Other sites like richarddawkins.net claimed the debate offered creationists credibility; hence, Bill Nye should not participate at all.

During the debate, Bill Nye argued that if America does not stop believing in God and start believing in science (again, suggesting God and science cannot coexist), we will fall behind the rest of the world. If that is true, then can you please explain how the United States, which started from nothing, has been the world leader for more than two centuries? Our cultural heritage is steeped in a strong belief in God, and it is only recently that we have tried to limit religious expression. As a matter of fact, up until the mid-twentieth century, evolution was actually prohibited from being taught in public schools, yet the United States has been the strongest, most productive, and most generous nation on the planet, and second to none with regard to our scientific advances. If believing God and the Bible are contrary to science and will cause us to fall behind the rest of the world, then why has the United States prospered so abundantly with such an emphasis on God? It is only recently that the United States is falling behind, which coincides with our culture's attempts to eject God and limit religious expression. This is no coincidence and has no other explanation. Try to explain that, Mr. Science Guy.

Depending on your convictions, the debate may not change your mind one way or the other, but it is available via the Internet.

> The unbeliever does not receive the things of the Spirit of God, for they are foolishness to him. And he cannot understand them, because they are spiritually discerned. (1 Cor. 2:14)

With all the money and resources being spent on atheism and all the efforts our politically correct culture is making to prohibit religious expression, you would think atheism has quite a following. As it turns out, less than 10 percent[14] of the population actually identify themselves as atheist. With fewer than one in ten people claiming to be atheist, why is our culture on its way toward eliminating religious expression? Why does political correctness require us to sacrifice the majority for the sake of such a small minority? This isn't to suggest that atheists' opinions don't count; rather, it points out the reverse: the opinions of the majority appear not to matter. There is only one logical explanation for this lunacy.

> For since the creation of the world His invisible attributes are clearly seen, being understood by the things that are made, even His

> eternal power and Godhead, so that they are without excuse, because, although they knew God, they did not glorify Him as God, nor were thankful, but became futile in their thoughts, and their foolish hearts were darkened. (Rom. 1:20–21)

What better scheme would allow Satan to function in complete stealth than convincing people there is no God? Indeed, if you do not believe in God, then you could conclude there is no Satan either. On the other hand, the more the world tries these pathetic efforts to suggest there is no God, the more convincing the prophecies in the Bible are about such attempts.

Sympathy for the Devil

> And no wonder! For Satan himself transforms himself into an angel of light. Therefore it is no great thing if his ministers also transform themselves into ministers of righteousness, whose end will be according to their works. (2 Cor. 11:14–15)

If Satan and evil are not manifestations of an ancient myth but are indeed real, how could you provide a makeover of his image so he could be more widely accepted and not feared? First, you would have to ask why you would want to do that. What purpose would it serve to try to convince people that Satan does not need to be feared, and more important, who would want to do that? After all, if you believe God is a mythical character, Satan would be as well, and if you believe in God, then you know Satan deserves no sympathy. Regardless of your religious convictions, Satan represents evil, or for you worldly folks, something really bad. Why would you want to do a makeover for evil?

Think about how the entertainment industry has portrayed Satan (and the occult) and how that image has changed over time. There are countless TV shows and movies that portray the occult in a positive light, some of which include *Charmed, Harry Potter, The Vampire Diaries, Ghost Whisperer,* and so on. Our culture goes as far as naming our places of business with occult terms, such as *Temptations,* and a few years ago there was a TV game show called *Greed* that glorified and exploited its contestants' greed for the sake of entertainment. Saul Alinsky even dedicated his book *Rules for Radicals* to Lucifer with this inscription:[15]

> Lest we forget at least an over-the-shoulder acknowledgment to the very first radical: from all our legends, mythology, and history...the first radical known to man who rebelled against the establishment and did it so effectively that he at least won his own kingdom—Lucifer.

The music industry has been glorifying the occult for decades. For example, the Rolling Stones produced and released an album in the 1960s called *Their Satanic Majesties Request*. A few years later the Rolling Stones released the hit song "Sympathy for the Devil," which sold millions upon millions of copies.

> He who sins is of the devil, for the devil has sinned from the beginning. For this purpose the Son of God was manifested, that He might destroy the works of the devil. (1 John 3:8)

As mentioned in the previous chapter, the Church of Satan was founded in San Francisco less than a month after the *Time* magazine article "Is God Dead?" Seriously, there is a living and breathing religious organization called the Church of Satan. Investigate it for yourself at www.churchofsatan.com. According to their website, there are nine satanic statements[16], which are as follow:

- Satan represents indulgence instead of abstinence.
- Satan represents vital existence instead of spiritual pipe dreams.
- Satan represents undefiled wisdom instead of hypocritical self-deceit.
- Satan represents kindness to those who deserve it instead of love wasted on ingrates.
- Satan represents vengeance instead of turning the other cheek.
- Satan represents responsibility to the responsible instead of concern for psychic vampires.

- Satan represents man as just another animal, sometimes better, more often worse, than those that walk on all fours, who, because of his "divine spiritual and intellectual development," has become the most vicious animal of all.
- Satan represents all of the so-called sins, as they all lead to physical, mental, or emotional gratification.
- Satan has been the best friend the church has ever had, as he has kept it in business all these years.

You may have also heard of the Wiccans. According to Wikipedia.org,[17] Wicca is a modern pagan religion that "was popularized in the 1950s and early 1960s by a retired British civil servant named Gerald Gardner, who at the time called it the 'witch cult' and 'witchcraft,' and its adherents 'the Wicca.'"

According to wicca.org,[18]

> Starting in the early nineteenth century, a new natural religion gradually evolved. It gathered momentum in the mid-twentieth century. Many authors and philosophers helped to develop the magical modern religion and to articulate parts of its belief structure. The religion finds its roots in ancient ways. It has psychic connections and sympathy with those who were burnt in the medieval period, and indeed with all individuals who have been oppressed and killed in the name of religion. The recent "festival" movement has enhanced the growth and diversity of the religion.

Wicca has a belief system that can be summarized in the eight words of the Wiccan Rede[19]: "If it harm none, do what you will."

Note that both satanically inspired organizations encourage self-indulgence and even go as far as arguing that sin leads to "physical, mental, or emotional gratification." If there is a God of the universe and his adversary, Satan, represents everything that is evil and wrong with the world, can you explain why someone would be compelled to create an organized religion in support of him and his agenda? The same question can be asked even if you believe God is a myth. Who would consciously choose to glorify a path synonymous with evil?

> For the message of the cross is foolishness to those who are perishing, but to us who are being saved it is the power of God. (1 Cor. 1:18)

While it departs a bit from the theme of this chapter, this next example takes the concept of Satan as being misunderstood to the extreme by making the assertion that religion is actually bad for society. In researching for one of the chapters in this book, I came across a video clip of Bill Maher making fun of Christianity in a stand-up comedy act. This seemed like a prime example of someone trying to convince people that God does not exist. Again, no God, no Satan. However, after a little research, it became apparent this was not his agenda after all. This research led to the discovery of the movie *Religulous*,[20] which might be characterized (loosely) as an anti-religion documentary of sorts. Toward the beginning of the film, Mr. Maher asserts, "Religion is a detriment to the progress of humanity," and while the movie strayed into other religions a little, the vast majority of the film was dedicated toward an anti-Christian focus. This decision to include other religions is actually a pretty clever attempt to further his agenda, but we'll get back to that later. Bill goes on to state that he was there "promoting doubt."

> For many will come in My name, saying, "I am the Christ," and will deceive many. (Matt. 24:5)

The film contains numerous references to cults, TV preachers, and essentially anything negative that the writers could claim to be connected with religion. Obviously, he was trying to associate some of Satan's best works as being representative of Christianity. He even included an interview with Jose Louis De Jesus Miranda as somehow being representative of Christianity. In case you have never heard of him, Mr. Miranda believed himself to represent the second coming of Jesus Christ, calling himself the "Jesus Christ man." Interestingly enough, Wikipedia.org[21] reports that he also referred to himself as the Antichrist.

> And Jesus came and spoke to them, saying, "All authority has been given to Me in heaven and on earth. Go therefore and make disciples of all the nations, baptizing them in the name of the Father and of the Son and of the Holy Spirit, teaching them to observe all things that I have commanded you; and lo, I am with you always, even to the end of the age." Amen. (Matt. 28:18–20)

In the film, Mr. Maher asks a person identified as a Christian, "Is heaven a better place than this world?" Of course, he was intentionally leading his guest into saying yes, after which he asks the follow-up question, "Then why don't you kill yourself?" Well, Bill, there are a couple of good reasons. Life is a gift from God, and second, the Bible tells us to make disciples of all nations. We are supposed to be living our lives for Christ, not killing ourselves for Him. As long as there are lost people like yourself, you can thank God that there are people willing to stand in the gap and pray for you.

Mr. Maher then strays into politics, posing quotes that imply that our Founding Fathers were not Christians. (Please read the chapter "Destroy Our Christian Heritage and Culture" to see the rebuttal to this ridiculous assertion.) Later, Mr. Maher tries to pick apart the Ten Commandments by asking why these ten rules are so important. He follows by stating that really only two of the ten are indeed laws (referring to "thou shall not kill" and "thou shall not steal"). Does this mean that he believes it is OK to treat your parents with disrespect, commit adultery, lie, and covet your neighbor's possessions? What do you think this says for Mr. Maher's character? But that is beside the point. If you are not careful, you will miss an important point in Mr. Maher's rebuttal. He refers to the sixth and eighth commandments as laws rather than God-given rights that are part of the founding principles of our country. If the rights to life and property are only laws created by men (rather than rights endowed by our Creator), then they can also be taken away by men. There is more on this topic later.

Mr. Maher attempts to challenge his Christian guests in several instances by trying to get them to admit that certain stories in the Bible were too outlandish to be true, such as the story of Adam and Eve in the Garden of Eden. Then if that weren't bad enough, he postulates that anyone that claimed to talk to God is indeed crazy. And by that he means insane. However, it is ironic that one of his next guests was Jose Miranda.

> But I make known to you, brethren, that the gospel which was preached by me is not according to man. For I neither received it from man, nor was I taught it, but it came through the revelation of Jesus Christ. (Gal. 1:11–12)

Mr. Maher further tries to challenge his Christian guests by asserting inaccuracies about the Bible. For instance, Mr. Maher claimed that the New Testament was largely written by authors that never encountered Jesus personally. This might be a good argument—if it were indeed true. The books of Matthew, John, James, 1 Peter, 2 Peter, 1, 2, and 3 John, Jude, and Revelation were written by either one of Jesus's apostles or one of His brothers, and most of the rest of the New Testament was written by Paul, who had a direct and very personal encounter with Jesus after His resurrection. Hebrews is the only book where the authorship is not certain. Therefore, only the books of Mark, Luke, and Acts actually fit Mr. Maher's assertion for the authors not encountering Jesus personally, which by the way does not make them any less legitimate. Let's see; that's three out of twenty-seven books. Now it seems likely that Mr. Maher is a pretty smart man, so what do you think the odds are that he knew what he was saying was inaccurate? If Bill Maher is on a crusade to get at the truth, why would it be necessary to lie? The only possible explanation is that he wanted to place doubt into vulnerable people's minds about the accuracy of the Bible. He couldn't say it in a movie if it wasn't true, right? Besides, what purpose would it serve to suggest that the authors of the New Testament did not know Jesus personally? Under this logic, only authors that personally experienced history would be qualified to write about it.

While the movie was heavily slanted with an anti-Christian focus, it did include a few short segments on other religions, including Judaism,

Mormonism, and Scientology, and he even threw in a cult that apparently achieves enlightenment through smoking marijuana. This was clearly an orchestrated effort to try to place all religions on the same plane, with none being better than the others; therefore, if one is bad, then they all are bad. You could easily argue that Christians comprise a majority of the population in the United States, but of all the countries in the world, which ones contain violence linked to religion? If you believe that all religion is bad for society, wouldn't it make sense to start with the real problems?

Toward the end of the movie, Bill Maher states that "religion must die for mankind to live" and goes on to assert that "religion is dangerous" and we should "grow up or die." He then appears to try to inject race into his argument by stating that "those that preach faith are intellectual slaveholders." He goes as far as seeking followers to join his crusade when he states, "Antireligionists must come out of the closet and assert themselves." Satan is calling his army.

But that is not the end of the story, and if you are not careful, you can actually miss a more important point. The movie spent most of the time trying to convince the viewer that religion was bad as opposed to supporting an assertion that there is no God. Based on the content of the movie, one might come to what seems to be a logical conclusion that Bill Maher is an atheist, right? On the contrary, there appear to be several quotes attributed to Bill Maher that contradict this seemingly logical conclusion. For example, Wikipedia.org states the following regarding Bill Maher's views about God:

> Maher is highly critical of religion and views it as highly destructive. He is described as an agnostic, and refers to himself as one in his feature film *Religulous*...As for labels, he has denied being an atheist, saying, "I'm not an atheist. There's a really big difference between an atheist and someone who just doesn't believe in religion."[22]

According to his own words, Bill Maher admits that there could be a God but somehow feels a calling to go on a crusade to abolish all religion, especially Christianity. The only difference between this view and Satan's view is that Satan knows there is a God.

> I saw [Satan] and did not recognize him...That is man's weakness and Satan's strength.
>
> —"The Howling Man," *Twilight Zone,* 1960

In the second season of the original series *The Twilight Zone*, there was an episode called "The Howling Man"[23] that provides a good illustration of the main point of this chapter. In this episode, Satan had been captured and was being restrained by the "staff of righteousness" and guarded by a number of dedicated keepers. The storyline includes a stranger coming to the castle that later discovers Satan restrained in a cell. Using lies and deceit, Satan desperately tries to convince the stranger that his captors are insane and he had done nothing to warrant his captivity. Satan eventually earns his compassion and convinces the stranger to release him despite dire and explicit warnings to the contrary. It was only after his release that the stranger discovers that the prisoner was actually Satan. In the wake of his guilt for releasing him, the stranger spends years in pursuit of Satan to right the wrong he had done. The episode ends as the stranger recaptures Satan, only to have another compassionate, misinformed character release him once again. Indeed, our inability to recognize Satan and his influence is our greatest weakness.

If Satan is synonymous with evil, why would you have sympathy for the devil? Why would someone start a religion based on Satan, the antithesis of everything good? Adherents would have to admit that either their religion is a fictitious manifestation of the founder's imagination or that they indeed represent everything evil. Why would a sane person choose this path?

You may wonder if Mick Jagger and members of the Church of Satan are actual agents of Satan. Because Satan is the master deceiver, it seems more likely that most of his followers are being misled and do not realize they are furthering his agenda. It seems unlikely that most people would be willing accomplices if they really knew his true nature and agenda.

Incrementalism

> Take heed to yourself and to the doctrine. Continue in them, for in doing this you will save both yourself and those who hear you. (1 Tim. 4:16)

> Since the general civilization of mankind, I believe there are more instances of the abridgement of freedom of the people by gradual and silent encroachments by those in power than by violent and sudden usurpations.
>
> —James Madison, June 6, 1788[24]

One of Satan's most aggressive strategies in use today is his attempt to destroy the Bible. He knows he could never eliminate the Bible outright, so he uses a strategy called incrementalism. If he tried to take the Bible away all at once, there would be such coordinated and passionate revolution, it would likely result in the greatest revival the world has ever seen. But what if he took steps to eliminate the Bible one verse at a time? The Bible is a big book, and you can afford to give up a passage or two without detracting from its message, right?

There is an unofficial term in golf called a mulligan that is used to cancel out a bad shot. It provides the golfer the option of not counting a really poor shot and allows a second try. While a mulligan is an unofficial term, it is customary among duffers to allow one per game. Well, how many mulligans do we get for the Bible? How many books of the Bible can we ignore? How many chapters? How many verses? If you believe in 70 percent of the Bible, is it still a passing grade?

> For the drunkard and the glutton will come to poverty, and drowsiness will clothe a man with rags. (Prov. 23:21)

According to cdc.gov—the website of the Centers for Disease Control and Prevention[25]—more than one-third of American adults are obese, and another third are considered overweight. This is a pretty frightening statistic considering the ill effects obesity has on the human body. Why is it so easy to play this game of Russian roulette with our bodies for such a fleeting pleasure? Regardless of your faith, the science is clear on obesity's detrimental effects to your health. Overindulgence is one of Satan's most effective temptations because we have not only allowed it; we have encouraged and embraced it.

> But I say to you that whoever divorces his wife for any reason except sexual immorality causes her to commit adultery; and whoever marries a woman who is divorced commits adultery. (Matt. 5:32)

In years gone by, there used to be a stigma associated with divorce, and it was something to be avoided. While the Bible does suggest divorce may be appropriate in certain situations such as adultery and abuse, marriage has gone so far as to become a disposable institution in our modern culture. Statistics show the divorce rate has been steadily increasing, with a sharp increase beginning in the mid-1960s. While some may take offense to blaming television for this trend, do you really believe that television doesn't influence our culture? How much has our culture emulated Hollywood as time progressed? As the rich and famous made divorce more and more commonplace, apparently so did our culture embrace it. Much of what we see on the television and the silver screen glorifies divorce and a promiscuous lifestyle. By making divorce mainstream, it is placed on the table as an acceptable option when a marriage is not going so well. Rather than being a measure of last resort, it is now considered an easy option. The point is not to suggest passing judgment on anyone that has been divorced; rather it is to show that it has become too easy and acceptable in our culture. Making divorce commonplace and acceptable is a brilliant strategy used by Satan to detract from the Bible while destroying the family unit.

> Flee sexual immorality. Every sin that a man does is outside the body, but he who commits sexual immorality sins against his own body. Or do you not know that your body is the temple of the Holy Spirit who is in you, whom you have from God, and you are not your own? For you were bought at a price; therefore glorify God in your body and in your spirit, which are God's. (1 Cor. 6:18–20)

> I say then: Walk in the Spirit, and you shall not fulfill the lust of the flesh. For the flesh lusts against the Spirit, and the Spirit against the flesh; and these are contrary to one another, so that you do not do the things that you wish. But if you are led by the Spirit, you are not under the law. Now the works of the flesh are evident, which are: adultery, fornication, uncleanness, lewdness, idolatry, sorcery, hatred, contentions, jealousies, outbursts of wrath, selfish ambitions, dissensions, heresies, envy, murders, drunkenness, revelries, and the like; of which I tell you beforehand, just as I also told you in time past, that those who practice such things will not inherit the kingdom of God. (Gal. 5:16–21)

In years past, we used to have a much stricter convention for sexual morality. While we were tempted, we lived in a society that placed boundaries on acceptable behavior. Even though we tried to push those boundaries, we were still expected to remain within them. Fast forward to today, our culture has not only abandoned the practice of abstinence; it appears as though it actually encourages sexual promiscuity to the point of suggesting you are in fact in the misguided minority if you are a virgin. Even our government-funded institutions where you send your children to be educated provide free condoms to children twelve years old and over in many states. While statistics vary depending on the source, it is estimated that almost half of teenagers, both boys and girls, have lost their virginity by the age of nineteen.

Again, how much do television and the movies influence our culture? What percentage of shows and movies do you know that promote abstinence or traditional family values? Can you even name a single modern series that does? Do you pay a service to bring this sewage into your home? Obviously, some of the first passages to get eliminated from the Bible (or at least ignored) are those relating to sexual promiscuity, and how easy it was for Satan to accomplish, especially with our assistance. Our culture has gradually moved further and further away from God's Will for our lives in this respect, because again we have not only allowed it; we have encouraged and embraced it.

> Before I formed you in the womb I knew you; Before you were born
> I sanctified you; I ordained you a prophet to the nations. (Jer. 1:5)

The next topic appears to be closely linked to the last one. Specifically, let's take a look at abortion, or the taking of innocent life. As of this writing, according to numberofabortions.com,[26] there have been more than fifty-eight million abortions in the United States since Roe vs. Wade. To put that into perspective, that is more than the current combined populations of the following states:

Louisiana
Kentucky

Oregon
Oklahoma
Connecticut
Iowa
Mississippi
Arkansas
Kansas
Utah
Nevada
New Mexico
Nebraska
West Virginia
Idaho
Hawaii
Maine
New Hampshire
Rhode Island
Montana
Delaware
South Dakota
Alaska
North Dakota
District of Columbia
Vermont
Wyoming

Further, there have been over 1.3 billion abortions worldwide just since 1980, which is greater than four times the entire population of the United States, and greater than the entire populations of either China or India. That is almost 20 percent of the current world's population. How many great leaders, scientists, and philosophers do you think have been included in that number? And if that isn't bad enough, ponder the irony and callousness of the following statement reported to have been tweeted by Planned Parenthood, the largest abortion provider in the United States, on the anniversary of the Roe vs. Wade decision.

"Happy 41st birthday, Roe v. Wade."[27]

The phrase was also the title of an article on www.feministing.com.[28] Truly, Satan is getting bolder and is no longer hiding his identity and true nature.

Proponents of abortion would argue that it is a right necessary to protect a woman's health. They also argue that abortions are justified in instances of rape or incest; however, less than one percent of abortions are reported to occur for those reasons combined. This means that the vast majority of abortions (more than 99 percent) occur for some other reason. Do you really believe it is morally acceptable to take a life just because it's not convenient to have a baby?

While we could argue for hours about when life really begins, anybody that would argue an abortion is necessary to save the mother in the third trimester is either a liar or an idiot. Further, who else but Satan would argue that killing a baby before it has been completely delivered is not murder? To suggest that a baby is somehow not yet human just because some portion of its body has not yet exited the mother's body is beyond absurd. As disturbing as that should be to anyone with a conscience, it actually gets even worse. In 2011, Kermit Gosnell was charged with the murder of eight persons including a patient and seven newborn babies reported to have been killed after delivery. In this particular case, a semblance of sanity prevailed and Kermit Gosnell was convicted of murder and was sentenced to life in prison without the possibility of parole.

But it gets worse still. The nation's largest abortion provider, Planned Parenthood, was in the news in July 2015 because their staff was caught on video discussing the sale of aborted baby body parts. Why are we allowing our tax dollars to support this immoral organization? Did you know that underage girls can get a taxpayer-funded abortion without getting consent from their parents? A young lady that is not old enough to vote can go into a clinic and have an intrusive medical procedure on her body that will terminate a life, all without having to get permission from a parent or guardian. Why would our government, an institution on the brink of bankruptcy, provide for such an immoral and expensive service, all the while encouraging disobedience to parents?

As a final note on abortion for those of you that still believe abortion is a woman's right, please take the time to view a recent documentary on the subject entitled *180.*[29] It is available via the Internet and provides a unique perspective in helping to understand the pro-life position. At the very least, you will have a better understanding of the pro-life point of view.

> Do not prostitute your daughter, to cause her to be a harlot, lest the land fall into harlotry, and the land become full of wickedness. (Lev. 19:29)

In July 2012, the United Nations Global Commission on HIV and the Law published a report entitled "Rights, Risks, and Health."[30] In the cause of controlling the spread of AIDS, the report concludes, among other things, that prostitution, illegal drugs, and sex with children should be decriminalized around the world. The United Nations, an organization of world leaders, has somehow come to the conclusion that legalizing these immoral behaviors would somehow benefit humanity.

Here are just a few excerpts taken directly from the executive summary of the report (pp. 9-10):

> To ensure an effective, sustainable response to HIV that is consistent with human rights obligations, the Commission forcefully calls for governments, civil society and international bodies to: …
>
> - Decriminalise private and consensual adult sexual behaviours, including same-sex sexual acts and voluntary sex work…
> - Reform approaches toward drug use. Rather than punishing people who use drugs but do no harm to others, governments must offer them access to effective HIV and health services, including

> harm reduction programmes and voluntary, evidence-based treatment for drug dependence…

Seriously, does anybody really believe legalizing prostitution, otherwise known as "consensual sex work" (*1984* doublespeak), will benefit our culture? The report asserts that if the trade were legalized, the government could regulate it, thereby reducing the chances for sexually transmitted diseases. The report has the same assertion advocating for legalizing drug use and sex with minors. They further claim that governments can reduce AIDS by providing hypodermics to drug users.

> Therefore God also gave them up to uncleanness, in the lusts of their hearts, to dishonor their bodies among themselves, who exchanged the truth of God for the lie, and worshiped and served the creature rather than the Creator, who is blessed forever. Amen. For this reason God gave them up to vile passions. For even their women exchanged the natural use for what is against nature. Likewise also the men, leaving the natural use of the woman, burned in their lust for one another, men with men committing what is shameful, and receiving in themselves the penalty of their error which was due. And even as they did not like to retain God in their knowledge, God gave them over to a debased mind, to do those things which are not fitting; being filled with all unrighteousness, sexual immorality, wickedness, covetousness, maliciousness; full of envy, murder, strife, deceit, evil-mindedness; they are whisperers, backbiters, haters of God, violent, proud, boasters, inventors of evil things, disobedient to parents, undiscerning, untrustworthy, unloving, unforgiving, unmerciful; who, knowing the righteous judgment of God, that those who practice such things are deserving of death, not only do the same but also approve of those who practice them. (Rom. 1:24–32)

One of the most ingenious forces attacking Christianity today is the homosexual lobby. (Note: This is not meant to suggest that homosexuals are bad people. The term *homosexual lobby* as used in this text is not intended to refer to homosexuals in general; rather, it refers to the angry, vocal, intolerant minority that is attacking Christians and Christianity. There is more on this in a later chapter.) While a relatively small percentage of people self-identify as homosexuals, just examine how much of our culture has evolved over recent years to pander to this minute sector of our population. In years past, homosexuality was largely treated as socially unacceptable behavior, and homosexuals may have even been treated as social outcasts. Fast-forward to today, homosexuality is not only considered acceptable, but it is celebrated and in many cases granted favoritism.

> Judge not, and you shall not be judged. Condemn not, and you shall not be condemned. Forgive, and you will be forgiven. Give, and it will be given to you: good measure, pressed down, shaken together, and running over will be put into your bosom. For with the same measure that you use, it will be measured back to you. (Luke 6:37–38)

The problem with the homosexual lobby is the manner in which they are infiltrating our society and demanding that Christians accept and approve of their lifestyle; otherwise we are treated as hateful and racist. In essence, they are demanding that Christians revise the Bible to redefine marriage and accept and endorse the homosexual lifestyle. To help illustrate the Christian perspective, consider the following scenario. The Bible states that having sexual relations outside of marriage is also contrary to God's Will for our lives. While Christians do not endorse those relationships, it should not affect their love for the people involved in them in even the slightest way, nor should Christians pass judgment on their actions. The same goes for a friend or a relative that might be of a faith other than Christianity, or even an atheist. Are Christians bigots for not embracing other religions?

If you want to make a permanent, long-lasting relationship with a same-sex partner, there is nothing to prevent you from that relationship. If you choose to include sexual contact in that relationship and it is within your beliefs, be thankful you live in the United States, where there is absolutely nothing to prevent you from doing so. On the other hand, don't be surprised and offended when Christians and many non-Christians alike do not want to fundamentally change the definition of *marriage* to something other than a bond between a man and a woman. If you want to have an honest debate about the issues, let's have one. But don't try to demonize Christians for adhering to a set of beliefs that has been the standard for civilized society for thousands of years. If you demand tolerance for your life choices, you can provide the same tolerance toward Christians. But of course we know that tolerance is not on Satan's agenda.

The homosexual lobby would have us believe that they are a discriminated and oppressed minority. They claim all they want are equal rights and protections under the law. Have you ever thought about what rights and privileges they feel they are being slighted that are only available to married people? Is it the right to free speech, freedom of religion, freedom to bear arms? Which of these rights apply only to married people? Which ones only apply to straight people? We could go on, but you get the point. The founders were incredibly smart about protecting our God-given rights, and they were extremely articulate in enumerating them into our founding documents. And just so it is clear, they apply to every law-abiding citizen, no matter what your sexual preference may be. Let's say that again so there is no misunderstanding. They apply to everyone.

Married people are required to pay a higher tax rate than single people. Could it be homosexual couples want to pay higher taxes? You may hear discussions about claims of benefits afforded to spouses by employers, such as health insurance, but despite what you may believe to the contrary, health insurance is an employee benefit, not a right. In fact, many employers already provide benefits to their employees and their same-sex partners without them having to be married.

When asked, the homosexual lobby will always provide a generic response that they want the right to government-recognized marriage rather than provide specific examples of those so-called rights that marriage is supposed to provide. Some examples of specific relational privileges/responsibilities that apply to married people include:

- visitation to the spouse in the hospital,
- property succession,
- parenting/legal guardian relationships, and
- retirement and Social Security benefits.

Extending these rights/privileges/responsibilities to homosexuals would not be a problem for most people. So if the specific privileges that they seek are not at all controversial, why don't they just ask for them directly? It is because Satan wants to corrupt the religious institution of marriage, so he is using marriage as the loophole to apply these laws differently than their original intent as the basis for his attacks.

> Therefore a man shall leave his father and mother and be joined to his wife, and they shall become one flesh. (Gen. 2:24)

Couldn't they solve their problem by simply having one of the partners identify themselves as the husband (the man) and the other would be the wife (the woman), regardless of their sex? But that would require us to fundamentally alter the definition of either *husband* or *wife* because a husband refers to a male and a wife refers to a female. Obviously, it would be ludicrous to change the definition of *husband* and *wife*, so why is it acceptable to change the definition of *marriage*? Since the beginning of civilization, it is clear that the definition of *marriage* includes the bonding of a man and a woman.

It is the government that has used the institution of marriage to define civil unions for the application of certain rights, including succession, parenting, property, and taxes. If you want the government to expand the definition of *civil unions* to apply to same-sex partners, you don't need to change the definition of the religious institution of marriage to do so. The same argument goes for employers who provide benefits to their employees' spouses. The businesses have used the institution of marriage to define the limits of their employee benefits, and they can choose to extend benefits to whomever they please. What if a widow decided she needed someone to share her life with, but for whatever reason, she no longer had an interest in sex? Perhaps her sister was in exactly the same circumstance and they have been best friends their entire lives. What if they wanted to create a permanent, exclusive relationship with each other that would provide the same relational privileges and responsibilities as married people? Would they have to get married to obtain that relationship? Why would our culture deny this perfectly logical and beneficial relationship? Again, if the specific rights they seek are not controversial, why is it necessary to change the definition of *marriage*? There is only one logical explanation.

If you really believe the homosexual lobby is only concerned with preserving the rights of homosexuals and not directed at undermining Christianity, then you are closing your eyes to overwhelming evidence to the contrary. The majority of the claims of discrimination by the homosexual lobby are specifically directed at Christians and Christian organizations. Their rhetoric accuses Christians of the exact same hate they are promoting themselves. In parts of the Middle East, homosexuality is treated as a crime punishable by death based on the precepts of Islam, so why single out Christianity?

Recall 1 Corinthians 6:9–10. If Christians are really so intolerant of homosexuals because of what they believe, then why aren't there similar efforts protecting the rights of the sexually immoral, idolaters, adulterers, thieves, the greedy, drunkards, the verbally abusive, and swindlers against their intolerant Christian oppressors? Christianity teaches us that all sin is equally bad, so it seems logical that Christians are also hateful to these other groups as well. While you are at it, you can also add in the mix every other religion because the Bible states that the only way to heaven is through Jesus Christ. Do you believe Christians are prejudiced against everyone that is not a Christian? Christians would not want to host a Muslim marriage ceremony in their place of worship any more than Muslims would want to host a Baptist marriage at theirs. Why doesn't the same standard apply? Where is the ACLU when it comes to protecting the rights of these other groups? The answer is very simple. At least for today, these other groups do not hold the same victim status that the homosexual lobby are able to portray for homosexuals.

There is no doubt whatsoever that some homosexuals have experienced varying levels of discrimination and even persecution in the past, and it may still be a very real threat in many countries (other than the United States). To suggest homosexuals are somehow a victim in today's American culture is absolutely absurd and to claim Christians are somehow responsible for this imaginary plight borders on insanity.

In order to provide equal time, let's take a look at a pro-homosexual documentary called *For the Bible Tells Me So.*[31] The premise of the film appears to suggest that homosexuality is normal/natural behavior. In this film the writers claim that numerous animals in nature have homosexual relationships, including "zebras, dolphins, baboons, sheep, buffalo, ducks, foxes, elephants, horses, gorillas, moose, cats, pigs, mice, rabbits, swans, and lions, to name a few." (Seriously, they really say that.) This so-called documentary uses dated film footage to show some people expressing prejudices aimed at homosexuals and implies that it is somehow representative of Christianity. But that is not why the film is mentioned here. This movie is presented as a documentary that is supposed to be providing convincing evidence to the viewer that homosexuality is a normal behavior and that it is not a choice but is somehow embedded into a person's genes. The movie provides example after example of homosexuals and how they became fulfilled after they started to accept who they were and followed an openly homosexual lifestyle. The movie even suggests that homosexuality can be explained scientifically. The writers go so far as to claim that when a male baby is in his mother's womb, the mother's body reacts negatively to the presence of the male body and develops a defense against it that causes the male to more likely be homosexual. They claim that the more male babies a mother has, the more likely one will become a homosexual. OK, then how do you explain lesbians? Apparently nobody thought to ask that question.

But seriously, that is still not the main point. This movie is a (so-called) documentary explaining the nature and (let's say) science of homosexuality. So what do you think the title of a documentary on the science of homosexuality should be called? While the casual observer might conclude this was a movie promoting and defending the homosexual lifestyle, in reality, it is a direct attack on Christianity. As previously noted, Christianity is not the only religion that teaches that homosexuality is sinful. Why do you think this movie was called *For the Bible Tells Me So*? There is only one logical explanation.

Don't fall into the trap of letting Satan convince you that because you are a Christian you are a racist. Do not be afraid to challenge his whole premise when attacked. For instance, there was a recent poster on Facebook that posed the question, "So you still think homosexuality is sinful and therefore gays should not be allowed to marry?" The poster then provides a flowchart for responding to the question. If you respond yes, then it follows through a serious of questions including Old Testament and New Testament references that eventually lead to accusing a Christian believer of being "sexist, chauvinistic, judgmental, and xenophobic." If you answer no, then it congratulates you for "being part of civilized society." If indeed you were inclined to examine the poster further, the great deceiver attempts to misinterpret the Bible by claiming the New Testament does not speak against committed same-sex relationships and further tries to discredit the apostle Paul's words by accusing him of being sexist through misinterpretation of the text. The most elusive part of the trap is the way they pose the question. Christians don't oppose same-sex marriage because homosexuality is sinful. Christians and non-Christians alike oppose a fundamental redefining of the religious institution of marriage.

> Another parable He put forth to them, saying: "The kingdom of heaven is like a man who sowed good seed in his field; but while men slept, his enemy came and sowed tares among the wheat and went his way." (Matt. 13:24–25)

Let's fast-forward to one of Satan's most ambitious conquests, infiltrating the church. The Presbyterian Church (USA) ordained its first openly homosexual pastor in 2011[32]. How many verses in the Bible did they ignore to make these things happen? How much of the Bible can we throw out the door and still be called Christians?

†††

> All Scripture is given by inspiration of God, and is profitable for doctrine, for reproof, for correction, for instruction in righteousness, that the man of God may be complete, thoroughly equipped for every good work. (2 Tim. 3:16–17)

Satan is systematically attacking Christian values one verse at a time to achieve his goal of incremental destruction of the Bible. He is using temptation and bullying techniques to get the weak and gullible to cave in. He is effective at tempting us with sin because, frankly, we have not only allowed it, but we have encouraged and embraced it. And whenever that fails, he can effectively shut down the conversation by accusing Christians of hate speech because our country has been so sensitized to the subject of racism. Are you going to allow Satan to bully and hoodwink you out of your Bible one verse at a time? When are you going to say enough is enough?

It appears that we are on track for a time when Christians will be unjustly accused of more and more intolerance in Satan's attempts to remove the good news of the Bible until it is so diluted, it will no longer be the same message. Be prepared to respond to the detractors with the loving Truth that we are all sinners in God's eyes and that Christians love the sinner and hate the sin. The only way to win this war against Satan is to stand firm, surrounded by the full armor of God.

> But I say to you who hear: Love your enemies, do good to those who hate you, bless those who curse you, and pray for those who spitefully use you. To him who strikes you on the one cheek, offer the other also. And from him who takes away your cloak, do not withhold your tunic either. (Luke 6:27–29)

DESTROY THE FAMILY

Destroy the family and you destroy society.

—(attributed to) Vladimir Lenin

The family unit—spawning ground of lies, betrayals, mediocrity, hypocrisy and violence—will be abolished. The family unit, which only dampens imagination and curbs free will, must be eliminated..."

—Michael Swift, *The Homosexual Manifesto,* 1987[33]

ANOTHER OF SATAN'S strategies prevalent in our culture today is his attempts to destroy the family unit. While we discussed divorce in the previous chapter as an assault on biblical principles, it is also a frontal assault on the family unit. Since we discussed divorce at length in the previous chapter, we won't spend a lot of time on it here; however, a symptom of divorce produces another direct assault on the family by making it perfectly acceptable to have children out of wedlock. Illegitimacy rates in the United States remained largely static at less than 10 percent of all births until the mid-1960s, when the rate began a steady and pronounced increase. The Centers for Disease Control published a study on births in the United States in 2012[34] that reported unwed motherhood remained near a historic high. Of the almost four million babies born in the United States during the year, over 1.6 million (approximately 40.7 percent) were born to unmarried women. Compare this to 1980 when only 18.4 percent of the babies born in the United States were illegitimate.

An article entitled "Rising Illegitimacy: America's Social Catastrophe,"[35] by Patrick F. Fagan, PhD, notes the consequences of this trend and the negative impact it has on the children and families (p. 3).

> From the very beginning, children born outside of marriage have life stacked against them. While many single parents work wonders and raise their children well despite the obstacles they encounter, for many others the challenge is too great and their children suffer the consequences.
>
> The impact on the child is significant and can be permanent. For many, out-of-wedlock birth and growing up in a single-parent family means the child is more likely to suffer from:
>
> - Poorer health as a newborn and, if his mother is very young, from an increased chance of dying;
> - Retarded cognitive (especially verbal) development;
> - Lower educational achievement;
> - Lower job attainment;
> - Increased behavior and emotional problems;
> - Lower impulse control;
> - Retarded social development; and
> - Increased crime in their community if there is a high level of illegitimacy.
>
> The root cause of these ills lies not in poverty but in the lack of married parents.

Mr. Fagan goes on to explain that while federal policy does not cause the problem, federal policy (welfare) does provide incentives for childbirth out of wedlock.

Whatever statistics you want to use, clearly the vast majority of couples enjoy traditional relationships, specifically between a man and a woman. So if homosexuals want to be equal, why is it necessary to oppose traditional marriage and violently persecute those who support it? The fact of the matter is that they don't want homosexual marriage to be equal to traditional marriage; rather, it appears that the ultimate goal is to eliminate traditional marriage altogether. Look up "Attacked by Tolerance" on YouTube and see the tactics of the homosexual lobby against those who support traditional marriage. Again, this is not intended to suggest that homosexuals are bad people; rather, it is to point out the negative tactics of the few trying to promote the homosexual agenda.

While homosexuals are trying to redefine *marriage*, there is another sector of the population that is reverting away from marriage altogether. In a *Newsweek.com* article entitled "The Case Against Marriage,"[36] the authors suggest that marriage is an outdated institution. The article states that "marriage is—from a legal and practical standpoint, anyway—no longer necessary." The article goes on to state that "most spousal rights can be easily established outside of the law, and that Americans are cohabiting, happily, in record numbers…and no longer need a marriage license to visit our partners in the hospital." If you claim that marriage is an outdated institution for the reasons cited in the article, wouldn't those same exact reasons apply to homosexual couples, and even more so? You can't have it both ways, unless of course you understand the real agenda.

Even our government is providing disincentives to marriage. An article on the Heritage Foundation website entitled "The New Federal Wedding Tax: How Obamacare Would Dramatically Penalize Marriage,"[37] describes how the new Affordable Care Act (aka ObamaCare) will penalize married couples. The article compares the government health-care benefits under the new law for both married and unmarried couples making identical combined income and goes on to reveal that some married couples would end up paying more than $10,000 per year more than their respective unmarried counterparts, depending on their income. The law even provides a substantial marriage penalty for low-income earners, although not as great. These penalties don't include the increased out-of-pocket expenditures for health-care services, which can be enormous depending on what services you need in a particular year. Why would the government penalize marriage when there are so many benefits to having strong families in our culture?

On June 26, 2015, the Supreme Court of the Unites States (SCOTUS) ruled five to four in favor of striking down the ban on same-sex marriage, thereby making it legal in all fifty states. Now that the definition of *marriage* has been compromised, it opens the door to all other kinds of perversions of the institution, including but not limited to:

- plural marriages (marriage to more than one spouse),
- marriage to family members (incest),
- marriage to animals, and
- marriage to objects.

Can bisexuals marry two partners? Homosexuals have the "right" to marry same-sex partners; bisexuals should be able to marry one of each.

†††

> Therefore I tell you, do not be anxious about your life, what you will eat or what you will drink, nor about your body, what you will put on. Is not life more than food, and the body more than clothing? (Matt. 6:25)

Unless you happen to frequently watch the *Jerry Springer Show*, there is another sector of the population that was mentioned earlier that many people may not be familiar with, the transgendered. This new word apparently applies to people who do not identify themselves as conforming to the sex they were "assigned" at birth. If straight versus homosexual was not confusing enough, enter those who do not believe themselves either completely male or female. So not only is our culture trying to redefine *marriage*; there are some that are now trying to redefine what it means to be male and female. (These are the same people who claim science is on their side). Most disturbing are the lengths these people are willing to undergo to obtain this gender disorientation. You might have thought it to be nothing more than superficial changes such as dress, makeup, possible lifestyle changes, and in extreme cases, surgical alterations. However, this is only part of the story. These individuals actually undergo sex reassignment therapy (SRT), including hormone treatments, to obtain some of the desired results, and as bad as this sounds, it actually gets worse. Parents are allowing their children to undergo this SRT at very early ages. There was an article the Dailymail.com[38] that reported about a young boy that was able to discern at a mere three years of age that he was supposed to be a girl. The article goes on to describe this condition as Gender Identity Disorder (GID). Some so called experts have even rationalize that withholding hormone treatment could be harmful to the child.[39] Let's say that again. They claim the SRT is for the child's own good. You can't make this stuff up.

Are you ready for the next dose of Gender Confusion 101? It is apparently perfectly acceptable to allow very young children to undergo hormone therapy, but only as long as it is contrary to the child's actual gender. What do you think would happen to that same child with gay tendencies that wanted to be straight? Wouldn't you think the child could get psychiatric help or at least counseling? There was an article on CNN.com entitled "California Governor OKs Ban on Gay Conversion Therapy, Calling It 'Quackery,'"[40] which reports that the governor signed a bill outlawing reparative therapy for GID. Let's get this straight (no pun intended). It is perfectly legal and acceptable to treat a child with powerful mind- and body-altering drugs and encourage the child into believing it is actually possible to change his or her gender, but it is not only unacceptable but illegal to counsel a child to help him or her with an identity crisis? The legislation that Governor Jerry Brown signed into law effective January 1, 2013, "prohibits attempts to change the sexual orientation of patients under age 18." It appears the world has finally flipped, and frankly, most of us are standing by and letting it happen.

An article on canadafreepress.com entitled "The State of California's Assault on Family Values Continues into 2012"[41] describes Assembly Bill 266 before the California legislature. The bill (if passed) would allow a pupil to decide what sex he or she wanted to be in order to compete in sports. The bill would also allow the pupil to decide which locker room he or she wanted to use. How in the world would you expect our educators to manage this problem? It is only a matter of time before there is no separation of the sexes.

Are you ready to send your kids to public schools where the boys and girls use the same restrooms and showers—together?

Enter news from the really weird. Germany recently established a third gender option[42] for parents filling out birth certificates for newborn babies. They can choose "indeterminate" if the child shows both male and female characteristics. Australia began to allow citizens to identify themselves as intersex on passports[43] and other documents, and in 2009, citizens of both India and Pakistan also gained new rights to identify their gender beyond male and female.

Why is it that our culture believes we are helping these individuals by encouraging and endorsing GID? Some sources suggest that transgendered individuals have a suicide rate twenty times greater than the average population. In a *Los Angeles Times* article entitled "Transgender Study Looks at 'Exceptionally High' Suicide-Attempt Rate,"[44] the author states that "a whopping 41% of people who are transgender or gender-nonconforming have attempted suicide sometime in their lives." Shouldn't that tell us something? You can't change your sex just because you want to. It is scientifically impossible. To help illustrate the irrationality of the transgender movement, consider another similar disorder for comparison. Apparently there are people who actually believe they are disabled individuals trapped in healthy bodies and are committing atrocities on themselves to obtain their desired results, including cutting off or damaging their limbs, eyes, ears, and so on. They are referred to as "transabled.[45]" Apparently these individuals believe their true selves were not meant to include a complete and healthy body, and they cannot be truly happy until they realize their disability. Is there a rational person alive that believes this to be a valid condition and that these individuals should be encouraged in achieving their desired handicap? At least with this condition, the person with the mental disorder can actually obtain the desired results.

Imagine, if you will, the next series of "trans" conditions. An obvious one that comes to mind would be "transracial," when people believe their true selves are a different race than the one they were assigned at birth. In 2015, the president of the National Association for the Advancement of Colored People (NAACP) chapter in Spokane, Washington, Rachel Dolezal, resigned after allegations that she had lied about her race. It was reported that she was representing her race as black, while she was apparently born of Caucasian parents. If it is acceptable to change gender, why would it not be acceptable to change your race? Why would this be a problem in today's politically correct culture? What is to stop a person from claiming he or she was meant to be another species (transspecies)? Can you imagine the new census forms and the additional questions required? Instead of having you select your race or ethnicity, the question would have to be revised to ask your ethnicity as "assigned at birth." This would be hilarious if it wasn't so sad.

> And you, fathers, do not provoke your children to wrath, but bring them up in the training and admonition of the Lord. (Eph. 6:4)

> He who spares his rod hates his son, But he who loves him disciplines him promptly. (Prov. 13:24)

The next example of the assault on families is the movement to ban discipline by parents by preventing the use of corporal punishment. For those not familiar with the term, *corporal punishment* refers to spanking. A brief search on the web reveals that forty-three countries already have a complete ban. The state of Delaware has also outlawed parents from using corporal punishment, making it a class A misdemeanor, and the state has already used the statute to put parents in jail.[46] While the intent of the law is to prevent children from being abused, the law's definition of *physical injury* states: "shall mean any impairment of physical condition or pain."[47] While the law may have good intentions, it does, nonetheless, place an attack on traditional Christian values, limiting a parent's rights to bring up a child as he or she sees fit. While child abusers should be punished, a parent should not be punished for loving his or her kids enough to provide correction. It is ironic that the same government that says it is illegal to spank your children allows you to terminate your child's life through an abortion.

†††

There is an article on patriotpost.us entitled "Helicopter Parents? Helicopter Government Is More Like It,"[48] which describes a similar encroachment on parenting rights. It was reported that Child Protective Services (CPS) in Montgomery County, Maryland, sought legal action against the parents of a ten-year-old and a six-year-old for the unspeakable crime of letting their kids walk home from school unsupervised. While the parents believed they were in the right, they eventually capitulated because CPS threatened to take their kids away. What parent wouldn't?

In another article on patriotpost.us entitled "Destroying the Family to Achieve Utopia,"[49] the author analyzes the "musings" of University of Warwick professor Adam Swift and his partner, University of Wisconsin-Madison professor Harry Brighouse. The article discusses the communist ideals of these two "egalitarians" and how they suggest families are responsible for many of the inequities in our culture. Their views suggest that it is unfair for parents of affluent means to raise and educate their children because there are other children not so privileged. They even suggest it is unfair for parents to tell their children bedtime stories because not all children have the same benefit. It was also suggested that parents should feel guilty about providing for their children's needs. They admit that these children do better than their less fortunate counterparts but suggest it would be somehow better for society to eliminate this familial inequity to produce equality in outcomes vs. equality in opportunities. Their utopian view includes making everyone the same, which can only be accomplished by reducing them to the lowest common denominator. The article goes on to quote Swift: "One way philosophers might think about solving the social justice problem would be by simply abolishing the family… If the family is this source of unfairness in society, then it looks plausible to think that if we abolished the family, there would be a more level playing field."

The destruction of the family unit is even extending beyond the home and being forced upon our educators. Specifically, it has been recently reported that an Oakland, California, school district has placed a complete ban on student suspensions for "willful defiance," which is described as "a broad category of misbehavior that includes minor offenses such as refusing to take a hat off or ignoring teacher requests to stop texting and more severe incidents like swearing at a teacher or storming out of class."[50] How in the world would you expect our educators to manage this problem? What possible good could this law produce? Why wouldn't you want parental involvement in these situations? The inmates would definitely be running the asylum.

It was a little difficult to classify this next example, which could have fit in a number of chapters or perhaps been another example in a chapter called "News from the Really Weird," but it does take the assault on the family to many different levels. Apparently, Washington state laws allow men to expose themselves to underage girls under the guise of nondiscrimination. In an article on theblaze.com entitled "'Non-Discrimination Policy' Results in Girls as Young as 6-Years-Old Being Allegedly Exposed to 'Male Genitalia' in Women's Locker Room,"[51] it was reported that a forty-five-year-old biological male has been allowed to expose himself to young girls while using showers because he identifies himself as a female. While the facilities are located on a college campus, the college rents the pool and other facilities to two high-school teams, which according to the article, results in girls as young as six years old using them. This obscene behavior has led to several complaints and police reports; however, Washington state law apparently allows this blatantly offensive conduct. Our culture has gone out of its way to protect someone with GID, but who is protecting these young girls from the harm and emotional stress that come from seeing a forty-five-year-old man's genitalia? Political correctness wins at the expense of innocent children.

> There is not an institution more vital to our nation's survival than the American family. Here the seeds of personal character are planted, the roots of public virtue first nourished.
>
> —Ronald Reagan, Proclamation 4845, Father's Day, May 20, 1981

The family is one of the pillars of society, and it is systematically being destroyed. We are slowing losing our sexual identities as we bow to political correctness. Marriage is on the decline, and illegitimacy and divorce rates are at a record high, all while there is an all-out assault by the homosexual lobby to redefine the institution of marriage. Let's face it: the single most effective thing Satan could accomplish to destroy society would be to destroy the family unit. The statistics clearly show how the decline in family values has resulted in more crime and poverty. Does anyone seriously believe that America will be a better place without families, where there is no sexual morality, if anyone can have sex with anyone else at any time and not worry about the consequences? Do you really want to live in an America where sexual identities are lost, where there are no distinctions between sexes, and life is disposable just because of convenience? Why would an intelligent person embrace these ideals that are so destructive? There is only one logical explanation for this lunacy.

Destroy Our Christian Heritage and Culture

If men are so wicked with religion, what would they be if without it?
—Benjamin Franklin to Thomas Paine

While revisionists would have us believe we are a secular nation, the facts just keep getting in the way. The next few pages contain a very small sample of the evidence proving our Christian heritage. Many of these examples and more can found on the Library of Congress website.

- "At its initial meeting in September 1774, Congress invited the Reverend Jacob Duché (1738–1798), rector of Christ Church, Philadelphia, to open its sessions with prayer. Duché ministered to Congress in an unofficial capacity until he was elected the body's first chaplain on July 9, 1776."[52]
- The Declaration of Independence, our founding document, states that all people "are endowed by their Creator with certain unalienable rights that among these are life, liberty and the pursuit of happiness."[53]
- At least nine of the thirteen original colonies had established churches, and all required officeholders to be Christians.
- Congress proclaimed May 17, 1776, as a "day of Humiliation, Fasting and Prayer" throughout the colonies. Congress urged its citizens to "confess and bewail our manifold sins and transgressions, and by a

sincere repentance and amendment of life, appease his [God's] righteous displeasure, and through the merits and mediation of Jesus Christ, obtain his pardon and forgiveness."[54]

- Congress set December 18, 1777, as a day of thanksgiving on which the American people "may express the grateful feelings of their hearts and consecrate themselves to the service of their divine benefactor" and on which they might "join the penitent confession of their manifold sins...that it may please God, through the merits of Jesus Christ, mercifully to forgive and blot them out of remembrance." Congress also recommends that Americans petition God "to prosper the means of religion for the promotion and enlargement of that kingdom which consisteth in righteousness, peace and joy in the Holy Ghost."[55]
- In 1777, the Continental Congress voted to spend $300,000 to purchase Bibles for distribution in the nation.
- On January 21, 1781, Robert Aitken presented a memorial (petition) to Congress offering to print "a neat Edition of the Holy Scriptures for the use of schools." Congress acted on September 12, 1782, by "highly approv(ing of) the pious and laudable undertaking of Mr. Aitken." The Bible contained the following Congressional endorsement:

> Whereupon,
> RESOLVED,
> THAT the United States in Congress assembled highly approve the pious and laudable undertaking of Mr. Aitken, as subservient to the interest of religion, as well as an instance of the progress of arts in this country, and being satisfied from the above report of his care and accuracy in the execution of the work, they recommend this edition of the Bible to the inhabitants of the United States, and hereby authorize him to publish this Recommendation in the manner he shall think proper.
>
> CHA. THOMSON, Sec'ry.[56]

- Congressional Thanksgiving Day Proclamation, October 11, 1782: "It being the indispensable duty of all nations, not only to offer up their supplications to Almighty God, the giver of all good, for His gracious assistance..."[57]
- The US Constitution includes the following text above the signatures: "Seventeenth Day of September in the Year of our Lord one thousand seven hundred and Eighty seven..."[58]
- On December 4, 1800, Congress approved the use of the Capitol building as a church building. The approval of the Capitol for church was given by both the House and the Senate, with House approval being given by Speaker of the House Theodore Sedgwick, and Senate approval being given by President of the Senate Thomas Jefferson.[59]
- Thomas Jefferson attended a church service at the US Capitol just two days after writing the infamous letter regarding the wall of separation between church and state. Jefferson attended church at the Capitol while he was vice president and throughout his presidency.[60]
- The east face of the apex of the Washington Monument is inscribed with the words *Laus Deo,* which means "praise be to God."[61]

If you are still not convinced, here are just a few quotes from politicians taken from various times in American history, including people who some would have us believe are atheists:

> While we are zealously performing the duties of good Citizens and soldiers we certainly ought not to be inattentive to the higher duties of Religion. To the distinguished Character of Patriot, it should be our highest Glory to add the more distinguished Character of Christian.[62]
>
> —George Washington, General Orders, May 2, 1778

> May every citizen...have a proper sense of the Deity upon his mind and an impression of the declaration recorded in the Bible, "Him that honoreth Me I will honor, but he that despiseth Me shall be lightly esteemed."[63]
>
> —Samuel Adams

And now I speak of thanking God, I desire with all Humility to acknowledge, that I owe the mention'd Happiness of my past Life to his kind Providence, which led me to the Means I us'd and gave them Success.[64]

—Benjamin Franklin, Autobiography

The belief in a God All Powerful wise and good, is so essential to the moral order of the world and to the happiness of man, that arguments which enforce it cannot be drawn from too many sources nor adapted with too much solicitude to the different characters and capacities impressed with it.[65]

—James Madison, November 20, 1825

The sacred rights of mankind are not to be rummaged for among parchments and musty records. They are written, as with a sunbeam, in the whole volume of human nature, by the Hand of Divinity itself, and can never be erased or obscured by mortal power.[66]

—Alexander Hamilton

But where says some is the king of America? I'll tell you Friend, he reigns above, and doth not make havoc of mankind like the Royal Brute of Britain....(L)et it be brought forth placed on the divine law, the word of God; let a crown be placed thereon, by which the world may know, that so far as we approve of monarchy, that in America the law is king...[67]

—Thomas Paine, *Common Sense*

The foundations of our society and our government rest so much on the teachings of the Bible that it would be difficult to support them if faith in these teachings would cease to be practically universal in our country.[68]

—Calvin Coolidge

> I am profitably engaged in reading the Bible. Take all of this book upon reason that you can, and the balance by faith, and you will live and die a better man.[69]
>
> —Abraham Lincoln

> As Commander-in-Chief, I take pleasure in commending the reading of the Bible to all who serve in the armed forces of the United States. Throughout the centuries men of many faiths and diverse origins have found in the Sacred Book words of wisdom, counsel and inspiration. It is a fountain of strength and now, as always, an aid in attaining the highest aspirations of the human soul.[70]
>
> —Franklin D. Roosevelt

Do you need even more evidence? The following are Articles from the States of Virginia and Massachusetts:

> Religion, or the duty which we owe to our creator, and the manner of discharging it, can be directed only by reason and conviction, not by force or violence; and therefore all men are equally entitled to the free exercise of religion, according to the dictates of conscience; and this is the mutual duty of all to practice Christian forbearance, love, and charity towards each other.[71]
>
> —Virginia Bill of Rights, Article 16, 1776

> It is the right as well as the duty of all men in society, publicly and at stated seasons, to worship the Supreme Being, the great Creator and Preserver of the universe. And no subject shall be hurt, molested, or restrained in his person, liberty, or estate, for worshipping God in the manner and season most agreeable to the dictates of his own conscience; or for his religion profession of sentiments; provided he doth not disturb the public peace, or obstruct others in their religious worship...[72]
>
> —Massachusetts Bill of Rights, Article 2, 1780

Certainly the evidence clearly supports that most of our leaders were steeped in the gospel and sought God's intervention in practically everything they did, including the execution of the public trust. While revisionists would have us believe the First Amendment prohibits religious expression, the text is obviously intended to keep government out of religion, not keep religion out of government.

To make this point, let's imagine that we went back in time and are participating in the drafting of the Constitution. For argument's sake, let's agree that it is our intent to prevent government-sanctioned churches and any attempt by government to establish laws governing religion. Further, being a deeply religious people, we try to live our lives for Christ in everything we do, and we want to be free to exercise our religion as we see fit. Government should not only be prohibited from making laws governing the establishment of religion, but they should also be prohibited from limiting the free exercise thereof. To be clear, we pray about everything we do, including the execution of the public trust. Being that we are very articulate people, we want to be exact and very clear in the language.

First, we want to be free to worship God in our own way. We don't want a government-established church that determines if, how, where, and when we worship. Let's see, how would we word this right with as few words as possible and be perfectly clear in the intent? Let's try this: "Congress shall make no law respecting the establishment of religion."

OK, sounds good, so let's put it to the test.

- Will it prevent a government-sponsored church? Yes.
- Will it prevent government mandating if or how the people would be allowed to worship? Well, partially. It would prevent Congress from making any law governing the establishment of religion, but:
- Will it prevent government from dictating when the people would be allowed to worship? For that matter, could the government prevent the establishment of certain religious beliefs? While it does prevent a government-established church, it doesn't appear to limit the government's authority to control some activities associated with worship.

If so, then government may still be able to prevent any church from doing certain things that it doesn't approve (like religious expression).

Sounds like we need a little more work to make this fundamental right just a little clearer. Let's try a slight modification:

> "Congress shall make no law respecting the establishment of religion or prohibiting the free exercise thereof."

Let's continue the tests.

- Did the modification result in any adverse changes in limiting government's ability to establish a state religion? None.
- Does the amendment limit the government's authority to establish when the people would be allowed to worship? Yes. It very explicitly states no law shall be established prohibiting the free exercise thereof.
- Being that we are a deeply religious people, we would like to be able to pray over our daily activities. Does the amendment prevent the government from limiting prayer? Yes. Again, it very explicitly states Congress shall make no law prohibiting the free exercise thereof.

Let's consider one more little change. Being that Christianity is the only true religion and the only way to reach God is through Jesus Christ, wouldn't it make sense to include prohibitions against any religion other than Christianity in our amendment? In fact, shouldn't the amendment mandate Christianity as a condition of citizenship? Well, the answer is simply no from several perspectives. First, in order to limit religion to Christianity, the government would have to define it. In order to do that, you would have to void the first part of the amendment, which prevents government from establishing religion. Secondly, prohibiting another religion is preventing the free exercise thereof; hence, you would void the second part of the amendment. Next, Christianity is a choice. Nobody can force you to become a Christian, and to try to do so would be contrary to biblical teachings. Finally, and most important, Christianity is the Truth and will always be victorious no matter the adversary (which is why there is such a significant effort to limit religious expression).

If you really believe that the founders meant for public activities to be void of religious references, couldn't that have been stated in the First Amendment more clearly? Do you believe our Founding Fathers, who were masters of the English language, would have overlooked such an egregious error? Couldn't they have added just a few words to the amendment to make it clearer (e.g., "respecting the establishment [endorsement (or) expression (or) acknowledgment] of religion")? The bottom line is they knew exactly what they were doing, and you can't deny it.

So what is this we hear about Thomas Jefferson's reference to the imaginary wall of separation? Contrary to what revisionists would have us believe, the words "wall of separation between church and state" do not appear in our Constitution. Thomas Jefferson penned those words in a letter to the Danbury Baptist Association in 1802 in response to concerns about the establishment of Congregationalism as their state church. Jefferson's infamous letter responded to their concerns by telling the Baptists that the First Amendment prohibited the national government from establishing a national church and concluded rightly that the Constitution prohibited the national government from interfering with matters of state governments. The following is an excerpt taken from Thomas Jefferson's letter. Please note the closing paragraph:

> Believing with you that religion is a matter which lies solely between Man & his God, that he owes account to none other for his faith or his worship, that the legitimate powers of government reach actions only, & not opinions, I contemplate with sovereign reverence that act of the whole American people which declared that their legislature should "make no law respecting an establishment of religion, or prohibiting the free exercise thereof," thus building a wall of separation between Church & State. Adhering to this expression of the supreme will of the nation in behalf of the rights of conscience, I shall see with sincere

> satisfaction the progress of those sentiments which tend to restore to man all his natural rights, convinced he has no natural right in opposition to his social duties.
>
> I reciprocate your kind prayers for the protection & blessing of the common father and creator of man, and tender you for yourselves & your religious association, assurances of my high respect & esteem...[73]

What is the strategy here? Because Satan cannot compete with the Truth of Christianity, his only option is to eliminate the competition by eliminating religious expression altogether. There is no other logical explanation.

> A good man out of the good treasure of his heart brings forth good things, and an evil man out of the evil treasure brings forth evil things. (Matt. 12:35)

Michael Newdow is known for a lawsuit he filed on behalf of his daughter, in which he challenged the inclusion of the words "under God" in the recitation of the Pledge of Allegiance. The Ninth Circuit Court found that the phrase violated the establishment clause because it constituted an endorsement of religion. While he lost the suit because he did not have custody of his daughter and therefore did not have the right to bring the suit, he filed a similar suit on behalf of other parents. Based on the previous ruling, the judge in the case determined that the Pledge of Allegiance was unconstitutional when recited in public schools. It was reported that he also filed lawsuits to prevent the invocation prayer at George W. Bush's second inauguration and to prevent references to God and religion for Barack Obama's inauguration. Mr. Newdow's motives are actually quite clear once you understand that he is the founder of the First Atheist Church of True Science (FACTS).[74] While an attempt was made to determine exactly what FACTS actually represents, their website had minimal information about its mission or purpose. However, if you want to do a little research and examine Michael Newdow's credibility, he makes it quite convenient with the posting of his "sermons." In one of his sermons, Michael Newdow discusses whether or not atheism is actually a religion. While *his* arguments are not particularly compelling, the tenets and adherents of atheism actually support that it is indeed a religion.

In an attempt to get more insight into atheists' beliefs, a question was posed on an atheist blog asking for the best evidence to support the notion that there is no God. Putting aside the adolescent, hormone-influenced, vile, and angry responses, the only reasoning anyone could offer was that there was "no evidence for the existence of God." But this does not explain atheists' beliefs. There was not a single response that could offer any sound *affirmative* evidence to conclude there is no God. Consider the three possible positions regarding a belief in a deity:

1. You believe there is sufficient evidence to prove the existence of God.
2. You believe there is insufficient evidence to support the existence of a deity.
3. You believe there is sufficient evidence to prove there is *no* deity.

For the first scenario, a person (theist) has been presented with enough evidence to conclude that God exists. While the evidence required may differ among individuals, a certain threshold has been met. The evidence is sufficient to conclude the existence of God, at least for that individual. In the second scenario, the person (agnostic) does not believe the evidence is of a sufficiently compelling nature and remains unconvinced there is a God. He or she believes there is insufficient evidence to support a belief in God. In the third scenario, the person (atheist) believes there is sufficient evidence to conclude that a deity does not exist. Think about this from a scientific perspective of trying to prove a negative. To help illustrate, suppose we asked the question, does life on other planets exist? A person who believes in UFOs might argue that there is evidence to support the existence of life on other planets. On the other hand, there is absolutely no existing hard evidence to support that conclusion. If you took the atheist's position in this case, you would conclude there is no life on other planets based solely on the lack of evidence, when in actuality there is no possible way to affirmatively make that conclusion. Therefore, if a person claims to be an atheist based solely on the lack of evidence, he or she is being intellectually dishonest because it requires faith.

Merriam-Webster.com's definition of *religion* includes "a cause, principle, or system of beliefs held to with ardor and faith." There is no possible way that a person could have sufficient evidence to conclude there is no God; therefore, atheism requires faith in a belief. We can then conclude that atheism is a religion. As a matter of fact, atheism is the textbook definition of a cult.

This then begs the question, aren't Michael Newdow's efforts to eliminate religious expression actually an exclusive endorsement of his own personal religion, atheism? In essence, he is using the First Amendment to endorse his own personal beliefs, something our forefathers were strictly trying to prohibit. If atheists got their way, the government would make laws establishing atheism as the official state religion and would prohibit the free exercise of any other religious beliefs.

The Declaration of Independence makes a reference to God with the phrase "endowed by a Creator," and our forefathers recognized that religion was so important that the First Amendment to the Constitution, the very first fundamental right of the people, included a very explicit acknowledgment for that right. In both the Declaration of Independence and the Constitution, the text acknowledges a belief in God. Isn't this an endorsement or at least an acknowledgment of religion that the Ninth Circuit Court ruled was unconstitutional? Apparently our Constitution and Declaration of Independence are both unconstitutional. You may find the whole concept a little humorous; however, it would not be surprising if indeed some court ruled that the Constitution was unconstitutional and decided to rewrite it. What do you think that revision would look like? Would it reflect our forefathers' wisdom in protecting our rights, or would it start to strip them away? You should be concerned because every time we allow this lunacy to continue, we are one step closer to losing our country and one step closer to slavery.

In the case of Engel v. Vitale[75] in 1962, the United States Supreme Court determined that it is unconstitutional for state officials to compose an official school prayer and encourage its recitation in public schools. There are countless other cases since that time where atheists have sued public entities for displaying religious references such as nativity scenes and other references to God. It is absolutely absurd that anyone could interpret the First Amendment as meant to limit a citizen's free expression of his or her religious faith (even for those who have government/public jobs). There is absolutely nothing ill that could come from the faith and tenets of Christianity. What part of love, joy, peace, patience, kindness, goodness, faithfulness, gentleness, and self-control would be a problem in a public forum?

If atheists truly believe that God is a figment of the imagination and has no basis in reality and therefore should be banned from being referenced in the public sector, then why don't they have the same irreverence about other imaginary characters? Should all of these symbols be banned from public displays? The only logical explanation is that Satan is using these willing and likely unknowing accomplices as a way to eliminate the Christian message.

In a document developed by the United States Department of Homeland Security titled *PROFILES OF PERPETRATORS OF TERRORISM—UNITED STATES (PPT-US),*[76] it is suggested that Christians can be placed in the same category as Islamic terrorists. On page 18 of the report, it states:

> There are five main varieties of religious terrorism: (1) Islamist terrorism; (2) Jewish fundamentalist terrorism, primarily inside Israel; (3) Christian terrorism, which can be further subdivided into fundamentalist terrorism of an Orthodox (mainly Russia), Catholic, or Protestant stamp (which, in the US, is especially aimed at stopping the provision of abortions) and terrorism inspired by apocalyptic Christian identity doctrine. (4) Hindu fundamentalist/ nationalist terrorism; and (5) terrorism carried out by apocalyptic religious cults.

Do you see the danger here? If you are pro-life and believe that an abortion destroys a human life, then your government may have a file on you as a potential terrorist and may possibly be infringing on your privacy under the guise of national security. Ideally Christians are not going to back down from what they believe, but you can imagine how this could shut down the debate between pro-life and proabortion groups. If you associate yourself with a pro-life stance, you could be putting yourself in danger of investigation and possibly harassment by your government. In the DHS's eyes, you could be treated no differently than the Islamic terrorists that destroyed the World Trade Center. This is undoubtedly leading toward that same goal of preventing Christians from sharing their faith. Just so it is clear, the bombing of an abortion clinic or the killing of an abortion doctor is in no way supported by the teachings of Christianity. God does not use evil for good.

In 2004, a bill was signed into law that adds sexual orientation as a protected category in Canada's genocide and hate-crimes legislation. While at first glance the reading appears reasonable in that it is aimed at preventing genocide, it also has a provision, Section 298 of the Criminal Code, that prohibits published matters that may expose a person to hatred, contempt, or ridicule. Because the Bible says homosexuality is a sin, it has been suggested that the Bible promotes hate and is therefore illegal. As a matter of fact, significant religious persecution is already occurring in Canada. The following text is a summary of the numerous examples of religious persecution cited in an article on campaignlifecoalition.com entitled "Anti-Christian Persecution & Oppression in Canada."[77]

> October 2003: The BC Human Rights Tribunal demanded a Roman Catholic men's organization, Knights of Columbus (KoC), awarded a lesbian couple $2000 for refusing to rent them their facilities for a same-sex wedding.
>
> December 2003: A British Columbia educator was cited for misconduct for writing a Christian article (while on his own time) and later suspended for appearing as a witness before parliament during the debate on same-sex marriage (SSM).
>
> June 2004: A Catholic church's tax-exempt status was threatened because of a letter written by their bishop pointing out that it was wrong for the church to support abortion and gay marriage.

September 16, 2004: Letters were sent to six hundred of Manitoba's marriage commissioners informing them they were required to perform SSM ceremonies or else lose their licenses.

November 3, 2004: A BC man alleges he was fired because of his beliefs on homosexuality and his refusal to rent KoC facilities for a SSM ceremony.

November 2004: The Saskatchewan Department of Justice instructs marriage commissioners they will be required to conduct same-sex ceremonies, regardless of their religious beliefs.

January 2005: Seven Newfoundland marriage commissioners resign after a judge orders all of them to perform SSM ceremonies or face dismissal.

March 2005: A gay activist filed a human-rights complaint against a Calgary bishop because of a letter he had written to his congregation outlining the church's opposition to SSM.

May 2, 2005: A Saskatchewan man was charged with alleged "hate speech" and ordered to pay $17,500 in damages for distributing a flyer in Regina containing warnings against the dangers of a homosexual lifestyle.

June 1, 2006: BC's Ministry of Education announced the mandatory inclusion of positive teachings about homosexuality for students in kindergarten through twelfth grade.

June 2006: A BC barbershop was vandalized after the owner opposed a homosexual pride proclamation during a city council meeting. The owner was also forced to apologize and pay $1000 to the gay activists.

February 2007: A homosexual activist filed a human-rights complaint against *Catholic Insight* magazine for "negative generalizations" about homosexuals while the activist's legal bills were covered by the taxpayer.

November 2007: The Alberta Human Rights Commission (HRC) ruled against a Christian pastor for publishing an article criticizing the goals of the homosexual political movement.

April 15, 2008: An Evangelical Christian ministry was ordered to cease using an employment contract containing a morality statement prohibiting immoral behavior including adultery, viewing or reading pornography, lying, and homosexual relationships. The ministry was fined over $23,000 for dismissing a homosexual woman who violated the terms of her employment agreement and was required to subject its entire staff to pro-gay indoctrination courses.

June 2008: Saskatchewan Marriage Commissioner was fined for refusing to marry two men based on his Christian beliefs.

January 2010: Ontario's Ministry of Education mandated a curriculum for both Catholic and public schools promoting homosexuality and masturbation as normal.

January 2010: The Hamilton-Wentworth District School Board (HWDSB) announced that parents will no longer be allowed to opt out their children from class when topics of homosexuality are brought up in the classroom, regardless of religious convictions.

While Canada's system of government is notably different, do you really believe the United States is that far behind? If our rights are not God-given, then they are human- or government-granted. If they are government-granted, then the government can take them away. If the government is powerful enough to take away the rights of one, then they are powerful enough to take away the rights of all. This is an incredibly slippery slope, and frankly, it may already be too late. Recall the cycle of freedom[78]: bondage to spiritual faith, spiritual faith to great courage, great courage to liberty, liberty to abundance, abundance to complacency, complacency to apathy, apathy to dependency, dependency back to bondage. The United States is clearly in the latter stages of this cycle. Even if you are still convinced there is no God, you should understand that liberty, once lost, is lost forever.

If you simply open your eyes, you can see the consequences of this trend to eliminate God. There have been numerous acts of evil in our country in the recent past, including the Columbine massacre, the West Virginia Tech massacre, the Aurora, Colorado, theater massacre, and more recently, the Sandy Hook Elementary School massacre in Connecticut. Our culture has systematically eliminated God from our schools, government buildings, and even our privately owned businesses, yet we are surprised when genuine evil takes a foothold. In a Fox News commentary following the Connecticut elementary school massacre, former Governor Mike Huckabee summed up this point very succinctly stating in part[79]:

> Well maybe it's simply the attempt to express our collective shock when we say: we are trying to make sense of the horrific shooting at the Sandy Hook Elementary School. But we're not going to make sense. Not from that which is totally disconnected from the cognitive capacity of any rational human being. The governor of Connecticut, Dan Malloy, got it right when he said "evil has visited this community"...
>
> On Friday, Neil Cavuto asked me, "Where was God?" And I said that for fifty years we have systematically attempted to have God removed from our schools, our public activities, but the moment we have a calamity, we wonder where he was...

> And I respond that as I see it, we have escorted Him right out of our culture, we've marched Him off the public square, and then we express our surprise that a culture actually reflects what it has become…

Without a doubt, Governor Huckabee nailed this one on the head. We have escorted God right out the door, and evil is taking over. How long are we going to listen to the politicians and mainstream media divert our attention from the real causes of these tragedies? How long are we going to sit and watch the dreams and hard work of our Founding Fathers being shredded to pieces? What about those who gave their lives defending liberty? Are we going to allow their deaths to be in vain?

> Live as people who are free, not using your freedom as a cover-up for evil, but living as servants of God. (1 Pet. 2:16)

As a short sidenote to this discussion, when was the last time you examined the one-dollar bill? The two circles on the back comprise the seal of the United States. Benjamin Franklin was tasked with developing the seal, which took a couple of years to design and a couple more to get approved. The seal has quite a bit of religious and cultural symbolism, which is summarized as follows:

- On the left circle of the seal:
  - the left side of the pyramid is unfinished, representing a nation that was just beginning;
  - the all-seeing eye represents divinity (God);
  - above the pyramid are the Latin words *ANNUIT COEPTIS,* which means "God has favored our undertaking"; and
  - below the pyramid are the Latin words *NOVUS ORDO SECLORUM,* meaning "a new order has begun."

- On the right circle of the seal
    - the eagle is holding the Latin words *E PLURIBUS UNUM,* meaning "out of many, one";
    - the thirteen colonies are represented several times, with thirteen stars, thirteen arrows, thirteen olives, thirteen leaves, thirteen bars on the shield, and thirteen letters in *ANNUIT COEPTIS* and *E PLURIBUS UNUM*; and
    - finally, thirteen stars are arranged in the shape of the Star of David.

Does this sound like the founders wanted to keep religious references out of government?

The Ripest Apple

> If I were the devil. If I were the Prince of Darkness, I'd want to engulf the whole world in darkness...but I wouldn't be happy until I had seized the ripest apple on the tree—Thee. So I'd set about however necessary to take over the United States.
>
> —Paul Harvey, "If I Were the Devil"

It is overwhelmingly obvious that the reason our nation has prospered so abundantly in the past 240-plus years is due to our founders' insistence on putting God first. There is no other logical explanation. That belief led to the most effective form of government ever created, a government of the people, by the people. So if the United States is a testament to the powers of God, can you imagine Satan's disdain for it? Take a moment to look up the commentary by Paul Harvey entitled "If I Were the Devil,"[80] which originally aired in 1965. Paul Harvey's essay articulately lays out the point of this chapter in a very entertaining and almost prophetic way.

Indeed, what better way to subvert Christianity worldwide than to destroy the United States? Consider how our country has drifted from a God-fearing nation to one that has not only shunned God but gone out of the way to eliminate any religious expression. How could we have strayed so far from our founders' intentions regarding our most basic rights? So, if destroying America would provide a significant blow to Christianity, what other strategies could we expect from Satan to undermine our country? Here are some possibilities:

†††

Step One: Eliminate our freedom of speech and expression, the very foundation of our country's roots.

Imagine if we no longer had the freedom of speech and the freedom of religion. The propaganda ministry would completely dominate our source of news in their attempts to control our thoughts, actions, speech, property, and everything else in our lives, exactly like Nazi Germany and Communist China. Any news that would cast a negative light on the establishment would be quashed and buried. For instance, most of us recall seeing the images of the man standing in front of the column of tanks in Tiananmen Square. Did you know most Chinese are not aware of this incident because they are not allowed to speak of it? You may know more about Chinese history than most of its citizens because the Communists control the media in their country.

But the government can't take away our liberties because they are guaranteed by the Constitution, right? Well, there is a bill called the Employment Non-Discrimination Act (ENDA)[81] that has been introduced in almost every Congress since 1994. According to the text of the proposed law:

The purposes of this Act are—

(1) to address the history and widespread pattern of discrimination on the basis of sexual orientation or gender identity by private sector employers and local, State, and Federal Government employers;
(2) to provide a comprehensive Federal prohibition of employment discrimination on the basis of sexual orientation or gender identity, including meaningful and effective remedies for any such discrimination; and
(3) to invoke congressional powers, including the powers to enforce the 14th Amendment to the Constitution, and to regulate interstate commerce and provide for the general welfare pursuant to section 8 of article I of the Constitution, in order to prohibit employment discrimination on the basis of sexual orientation or gender identity.

This is actually pretty scary because it could be used to force religious institutions to hire homosexuals, including clergy. However, proponents of the bill will argue there is an exemption for religious organizations. Section 6 of the bill states:

> SEC. 6. EXEMPTION FOR RELIGIOUS ORGANIZATIONS.
> This Act shall not apply to a corporation, association, educational institution, or society that is exempt from the religious discrimination provisions of title VII of the Civil Rights Acts of 1964 pursuant to section 702(a) or 703(e)(2) of such Act (42 U.S.C. 2000e-1(a); 2000e-2(e)(2)).

As proposed, the act specifically does not apply to religious organizations, but what if you have a private Christian-based for-profit business such as a Christian publishing company or wedding chapel? Then guess what! The government can force you to hire someone who does not have Christian values. But at least the bill protects churches from having to hire homosexual clergy and staff, right? At first reading, it certainly appears so, but let's read on. Section 16 of the bill contains what is called a severability clause that states:

> SEC. 16. SEVERABILITY.
> If any provision of this Act, or the application of the provision to any person or circumstance, is held to be invalid, the remainder of this Act and the application of the provision to any other person or circumstances shall not be affected by the invalidity.

This clause means that if someone challenges one section as unconstitutional, the remainder of the bill remains in effect. So if the religious exemption in Section 6 is found to be unconstitutional, then churches would no longer be immune. There is also a section in the bill that serves as a penalty for the losing party when enforcing its provisions. It basically says that the loser pays for the attorney fees and those of expert witnesses on both sides:

> SEC. 12. ATTORNEYS' FEES.
> Notwithstanding any other provision of this Act, in an action or administrative proceeding for a violation of this Act, an entity

> described in section 10(a) (other than paragraph (4) of such section), in the discretion of the entity, may allow the prevailing party, other than the Commission or the United States, a reasonable attorney's fee (including expert fees) as part of the costs. The Commission and the United States shall be liable for the costs to the same extent as a private person.

In theory, this provision is actually good because it should help discourage frivolous lawsuits. However, in today's politically correct society, do you really believe the courts will be fair and impartial? How many times have we heard of rulings being overturned by judicial fiat? The monetary threat to Christians and Christian businesses could be overwhelming to the point that people may eventually be prohibited from having any religious expression. The passage of this bill could eventually lead to a direct assault on Christianity and the destruction of organized religion. Satan would have direct access to attacking churches from within, backed by intrusive government intervention. The agents of Satan are already controlling the chaplains in our military and are actively persecuting[82,83] these Christian leaders for doing the job they were hired to do. Controlling religion in the military is a stepping-stone toward making such control mainstream.

There are already numerous examples of Christians that have chosen not to take part in homosexual civil unions because of their religious convictions and have suffered persecution by the courts, the government, and the public. Some of the persecutions were so severe, they even lost their businesses. In an article on the *Patriotpost.us* entitled "Tolerating Radical Islam but Not Christian Bakers,"[84] the author cites a quote from Alliance Defending Freedom Attorney Kristen Waggoner in reference to a recent judgment against a baker that refused to participate in a homosexual wedding. The attorney summed up the homosexual agenda very well when she stated, "The ruling basically said that if you dare to not celebrate same-sex marriage because it violates your religious convictions, that the government has a right to bring about your personal and professional ruin…" Did you get the significance of her statement? She did not say it would result in a correction of the alleged wrong, but rather, a destruction of the individual.

Step Two: Control public opinion through manipulation of the press.

There is a term referred to as the "Big Lie," which was taken from Adolf Hitler's book *Mein Kampf.* It refers to a concept that the bigger the lie is, the more likely it is to be believed: "because the broad masses of a nation are always more easily corrupted in the deeper strata of their emotional nature than consciously or voluntarily; and thus in the primitive simplicity of their minds they more readily fall victims to the big lie than the small lie, since they themselves often tell small lies in little matters but would be ashamed to resort to large-scale falsehoods..."[85] This precept was perfected into a science during Joseph Goebbels's tenure as the head of Hitler's propaganda ministry. He is the person attributed to saying that if you repeat a lie often enough, people will believe it. Joseph Goebbels believed the purpose of political speech is to persuade and admitted that the ends justify the means.

> He who is faithful in what is least is faithful also in much; and he who is unjust in what is least is unjust also in much. (Luke 16:10)

Likewise, the news media in America today show an incredible and blatantly obvious lack of impartiality. There are so many examples they would be another book in themselves. Suffice it to say, politicians continue to lie, cheat, and steal from the masses, all in the guise of taking care of us, which in reality only strengthens their hold on power, and the mainstream media continue to fail to call them out. This is not to suggest that all politicians and reporters are bad; rather, it just points out the magnitude of the problem. You will know them by their fruits.

Step Three: Bankrupt the country through fiscal irresponsibility.

> And He said to them, "Take heed and beware of covetousness, for one's life does not consist in the abundance of the things he possesses." (Luke 12:15)

> Therefore if you have not been faithful in the unrighteous mammon, who will commit to your trust the true riches? And if you have not been faithful in what is another man's, who will give you what is your

> own? No servant can serve two masters; for either he will hate the one and love the other, or else he will be loyal to the one and despise the other. You cannot serve God and mammon. (Luke 16:11–13)

Our politicians currently spend about $1.50 for every $1 in revenue they bring in. Some have even suggested that taxes are not high enough and the public is not doing their fair share. Because the bottom 50 percent of wage earners pay little to no income tax, this may be a true statement, but unfortunately the politicians end up making that gap even greater when given the chance. When they do get a tax increase, rather than paying off the deficit, they simply start new spending programs to benefit themselves and their constituencies. The biggest mystery is the vast number of Americans that don't recognize this as a problem, although, as George Bernard Shaw once said, "A government that robs Peter to pay Paul can always count on the support of Paul."

> If ye love wealth better than liberty, the tranquility of servitude better than the animating contest of freedom, go home from us in peace. We ask not your counsels or arms. Crouch down and lick the hands which feed you. May your chains set lightly upon you, and may posterity forget that ye were our countrymen.[86]
>
> —Samuel Adams

As a sidenote and bit of trivia about our fiscal responsibility, contemplate the following. A stack of one trillion one-dollar bills (stacked one on top of the other, each one 0.0044 inch thick) would reach over sixty-nine thousand miles, or approximately one-fourth of the distance from the earth to the moon (approximately 239,000 miles). We are not talking about bills laid end-to-end; this is stacked one on top of the other. That sounds hard to believe, so for the skeptics, here is the calculation: (1,000,000,000,000 bills x 0.0044 inches/bill divided by 12 inches/foot divided by 5,280 feet/mile = 69,444.44 miles). Our national debt as of the date of this writing is over $18,000,000,000,000. Our current deficit in stacked one-dollar bills would be enough for a trip to the moon and back—twice. The population of the United States is currently around three hundred fifteen million, which means our country has accumulated a debt of over $57,000 per man, woman, and child living in the United States, and the debt is growing exponentially. If our politicians are not held accountable, they can print money anytime they want, and they don't think the debt is a problem, then what incentive do they have to stop? Eventually the US dollar is going to be worthless, and at some point, this house of cards is going to fall. What do you think the failing of our currency will do to the United States and our way of life? These attacks on our financial security are no accident but a brilliant plan to bring about the end of the American way of life.

Did you know that the perpetual printing of fiat currency is a major driver of inflation? When money becomes less valuable through inflation, the amount of our debt becomes less of a burden because the amount a dollar would buy at the time the debt was accumulated was far greater than it is now. Even though we may pay interest on the debt, the value of that money is far less than it used to be, so in effect the amount that is paid back will be far less than what was borrowed. To aid in the scam, the power brokers manipulate what they say is the official current rate of inflation. This is because there are cost-of-living adjustments (COLA) for entitlements. If they claim the inflation is low, then the corresponding COLA is also low. In effect, they are decreasing benefits for these entitlements through inflation of the dollar.

Step Four: Destroy personal freedoms under the guise of taking care of the people.

> Of all tyrannies, a tyranny exercised for the good of its victims may be the most oppressive. It may be better to live under robber barons than under omnipotent moral busybodies. The robber baron's cruelty may sometimes sleep, his cupidity may at some point be satiated; but those who torment us for our own good will torment us without end, for they do so with the approval of their consciences.
>
> —C. S. Lewis, *God in the Dock: Essays on Theology and Ethics* [87]

The president of the United States' former chief of staff Rahm Emanuel once said, "You never want a serious crisis to go to waste…This crisis provides the opportunity for us to do things that you could not do before."[88] Consider the countless new laws and regulations that are being proposed and put into place to try to solve even the smallest problem. These laws are being sold as solutions to our problems but in many instances nip away at our God-given rights. Further, there are conspiracy theories out there suggesting that governments manufacture at least some of these crises, termed "false flags."[89] The theory suggests that governments will purposely manufacture a crisis in order to manipulate public opinion. In fact, Hitler used attacks on his own people[90] to gain their support for his twisted agenda.

> But He, knowing their thoughts, said to them: "Every kingdom divided against itself is brought to desolation, and a house divided against a house falls." (Luke 11:17)

A Google search on "how to destroy America" revealed several websites that referenced a speech by Richard Lamm, former governor of Colorado, that included eight steps to destroy America. In summary, those steps include the following:

1) America must become a bilingual country so that there are competing cultures.
2) Encourage immigrants to maintain their own cultures rather than be the melting pot we once were.
3) Celebrate diversity.
4) Make the fastest-growing demographic the least educated.
5) Have big business and government encourage and support these efforts with lots of money.
6) Establish dual citizenship and promote divided loyalties.

7) Establish taboos against challenging these activities.
8) Ban the Victor Hanson Davis book *Mexifornia* because it exposes the elements of the plan.

Dr. Ben Carson gave a speech to an audience at the Conservative Political Action Conference (CPAC) in which he outlined four similar strategies for destroying America. They include: [91]

1) Create as much division in the country as possible because "a house divided cannot stand."
2) Encourage a culture of ridicule for basic morality and the principles that made and sustain this country.
3) Undermine the financial stability of the country.
4) Weaken our military and destroy its morale.

Think about how the press has fanned the flames of division in recent years. You may be familiar with a news story regarding the death of a fifteen-year-old African American who was shot while attacking a Hispanic American in Florida (George Zimmerman). Despite the overwhelming evidence that the African American was shot in self-defense, the media latched onto this story and made a circus out of the entire affair. The media purposely distorted the facts and tried to make the death appear as though the shooting was racially motivated. One of the news media outlets shamefully and deliberately edited the 911 tapes so as to suggest Mr. Zimmerman had racial tendencies. Why would the news media deliberately distort the news of a story unless they had ulterior motives? And if that wasn't bad enough, there was a new term invented by the media in which they labeled Mr. Zimmerman a "white-Hispanic." Despite the media's attempts to distort the facts of the case, the evidence was clear that the shooting was in self-defense. As a matter of fact, the police chief refused to make an arrest because he knew there was no case. However, because the circumstances were so politically charged, the police chief was eventually fired for refusing to arrest and prosecute the man. Nonetheless, Mr. Zimmerman was eventually arrested and tried for the murder of his attacker, and the entire episode was covered 24–7 in a media circus that would rival that of Barnum and Bailey. Because the evidence was so clearly obvious in this case, sanity eventually prevailed despite the overwhelming pressures to cave into political correctness and the media's desire to burn this man at the stake of public opinion. Even the prosecution knew they did not have a case and, toward the end of the trial, tried to change the charge against Mr. Zimmerman to manslaughter. Even this pathetic attempt failed.

While racial tensions do exist in this country, evidence suggests that they are the exception rather than the rule, contrary to what the media and some politicians would have us believe. And with that said, try to put your favorite leaders to the test. Specifically, have they ever done anything to help elevate you from your circumstances, or do they derive their power by fanning the flames, of division and keeping you in those circumstances, thereby guaranteeing their continued existence in power? If you believe we are a racist nation, why is that so? Is it based on what you have experienced firsthand, or what you perceived because someone else led you to believe it? Do you judge people according to the groups he or she associates with (i.e., labels), or do you judge a person by the content of his or her character?

Do you see any trends in our culture? Why is it OK to celebrate every single diversity and lifestyle except Christianity? Why do we celebrate and emphasize the minority at the expense of the majority? Why does political correctness demand we celebrate our differences rather than celebrate and embrace the things we have in common? After all, we are indeed all members of the same race, the human race. Instead of being hyphenated Americans, why can't we just be Americans?

> When in the Course of human events, it becomes necessary for one people to dissolve the political bands which have connected them with another, and to assume among the powers of the earth, the separate and equal station to which the Laws of Nature and of Nature's God entitle them, a decent respect to the opinions of mankind requires that they should declare the causes which impel them to the separation.

> We hold these truths to be self-evident, that all men are created equal, that they are endowed by their Creator with certain unalienable Rights, that among these are Life, Liberty and the pursuit of Happiness…
>
> —Declaration of Independence, July 4, 1776

As mentioned, there have been suggestions that we need to rewrite our founding documents because the references to God and a Creator are unconstitutional. What do you think those revisions would look like? It certainly appears that America is moving further and further away from the rule of law toward a rule of men. But if we give politicians the power to take away the freedoms of others, then we are also giving them the power to take away our freedoms as well. Those who would manipulate you into empowering them at the expense of your freedoms will toss you aside the instant that power is achieved. But then again, that is the purpose of "useful idiots.[92]"

As a final thought, think about how our country will be affected with the weakening of our military and the destroying of morale. In an article entitled "Pentagon: Religious Proselytizing Is Not Permitted,"[93] Todd Starnes notes that the "Military Religious Freedom Foundation is calling on the Air Force to enforce a regulation that they believe calls for the court martial of any service member caught proselytizing." The article goes on to quote the President of MRFF, Mikey Weinstein, saying that he "said US troops who proselytize are guilty of sedition and treason and should be punished—by the hundreds if necessary—to stave off what he called a 'tidal wave of fundamentalists.' He went on further to say that 'until the Air Force or Army or Navy or Marine Corps punishes a member of the military for unconstitutional religious proselytizing and oppression, we will never have the ability to stop this horrible, horrendous, dehumanizing behavior.'" Mr. Weinstein believes religious expression is dangerous and should not only be stopped, but that servicemen and women should also be punished for proselytizing. Is this the America that so many men and women have died for? Is this the America that was envisioned by our founders?

†††

In the last several decades, we have been incrementally and systematically cutting God out of every aspect of our culture and replacing Him with a faith in government. In doing so our country has suffered tremendously. These actions have resulted in a decline in moral values, perpetual debt, and an ever-increasing dependence on the state, just to name a few. What better way to subvert God's influence worldwide than to destroy the United States and all that it stands for? It would truly be Satan's greatest conquest. Beware, however; if the United States ever loses its world leadership role, it will *never* be regained. Regardless of whether or not you believe in God, the fact of the matter is, the vast majority of people do. Religion (particularly Christianity) is a very real part of our culture. If you believe we should limit religious expression, then you believe in limiting free speech, but without free speech, we would not be a free society. You need to be tolerant of Christians and respectful of their beliefs in the same manner that you expect others to be tolerant of yours. Do you really want to forfeit some of your freedoms so someone cannot pray in public?

> If My people who are called by My name will humble themselves, and pray and seek My face, and turn from their wicked ways, then I will hear from heaven, and will forgive their sin and heal their land. (2 Chron. 7:14)

DHIMMITUDE

THIS NEXT OBSERVATION should absolutely scare the pants off any freedom-loving American regardless of his or her religious beliefs. Specifically, the First Amendment to the Constitution is being used to force Americans to violate their religious beliefs, that is, unless you are of a faith other than Christian. Here are a just a few examples.

We have all heard of various dating services, from computer dating to newspaper ads to postings on Craigslist. Have you have ever heard of eHarmony? Neil Clark Warren, a Christian theologian, is the founder and chairman of eHarmony. While the company had its beginnings marketing primarily to Christian singles, that policy eventually changed. In an August 17, 2005, interview on NPR[94], Warren responded to questions about his decision not to include homosexual dating services. While you would think a Christian theologian could cite Scripture regarding homosexuality as being contrary to God's Will, he actually responded to the question with a politically correct answer by stating that he had no experience in matching homosexual couples. Even such a worldly response did not protect him from the lawsuits that were to come. The first lawsuit against eHarmony was filed in 2007 based on a California law that businesses cannot discriminate against people based on sexual orientation. While the lawsuit was unsuccessful, eHarmony did make some changes. Specifically, a parallel dating service called Compatible Partners was created to serve the gay and lesbian community. Nonetheless, they were sued again in 2010 because detractors claimed that equal but separate was an abomination reminiscent of the 1960s.

First, let's examine the original 2007 lawsuit in which it was claimed that a customer was discriminated against based on her sexual orientation. This person had full access to eHarmony's site and was, in fact, not denied services; rather, the customer was demanding the company provide a service they did not offer, one in which they claimed they had no experience or expertise. Why would you go to a business and demand a service they have no expertise in providing? Persons seeking specific goods or services go to places of business that cater to their needs. There are plenty of homosexual dating sites available, so there is not a chance this person was actually injured by eHarmony's business practices. Can you imagine going into a Chick-fil-A and ordering a Big Mac? What if a Jew (or a Muslim) owned a restaurant, and as you know, it would be against their religion to serve pork. What if a person came into the restaurant and demanded pork chops? Under that same rationale, couldn't the customer claim that the owners are discriminating against his or her choices based on religious beliefs? How are these scenarios any different?

So why was eHarmony sued in 2010 if they provided a comparable service to cater to homosexuals? The homosexual lobby wanted this Christian businessman to provide a service that he did not offer, and when he did, they demanded that homosexual dating site appear to be the same as traditional dating. This was because their goal is to indoctrinate Americans into believing the homosexual lifestyle is mainstream, thereby watering down biblical principles and the family unit. Under their logic, the sexual preference of the applicant would be irrelevant. If sex does not matter, then the only thing that does matter is whether or not they are compatible. Imagine a time in the not-too-distant future where you could be sued for declining a same-sex date as matched by one of these dating sites. As a heterosexual, suppose you entered your profile into the system, pressed the button, and only got same-sex results. If you reject potential matches based on sex and your religious convictions, there may come a time that you could be sued.

In another example, a woman in California sued her doctor after the doctor refused to provide an in vitro procedure because of her religious convictions[95]. Despite the fact that the patient was referred to another doctor that would provide the exact same procedure, the patient still sued the doctor for discrimination. Again, this person was not denied anything and appears to be 100 percent about attacking the doctor's Christian values. California's highest court ruled in favor of the plaintiff, barring doctors from invoking their religious beliefs as a reason for denying treatment to gays and lesbians. The ruling asserts that state law prohibiting discrimination based on sexual orientation extends to the medical profession. The article stated that the suit was settled for an undisclosed amount of money, which was nothing less than a tax on Christian beliefs. So, can a doctor be sued for not providing an abortion? Such a case is surely coming.

Irrespective of your constitutional right to free exercise of religion, the government is now encroaching on what religious expressions you can have. Imagine you are a Christian pastor with traditional values, and a homosexual couple wants you to marry them and they want to use your church and services contrary to your Christian beliefs. Despite the fact that there are countless places for the couple to be united and countless clergy that would perform the ceremony, you may be targeted simply because of your Christian beliefs and convictions. If you follow your beliefs, you get sued. If you perform the ceremony, you risk losing credibility as a Christian minister. In an article dated October 18, 2014, on dailysignal.com entitled "Government to Ordained Ministers: Celebrate Same-Sex Wedding or Go to Jail,"[96] it was reported that an Idaho couple is facing just such a persecution. The couple runs a for-profit wedding chapel, and they are both ordained ministers. Because the chapel is a for-profit business, the city determined it to be a public accommodation and therefore a nondiscrimination statute applies. In short, these ordained ministers of the gospel were told they had to celebrate same-sex weddings or face fines and possible jail time.

Recently, a retail craft store chain, Hobby Lobby, made the news because of their lawsuit to challenge the Affordable Care Act, which requires providing emergency contraception. In a letter from David Green, CEO and founder of Hobby Lobby, he writes in part:

> So, Hobby Lobby and my family are forced to make a choice. With great reluctance, we filed a lawsuit today, represented by the Becket Fund for Religious Liberty, asking a federal court to stop this mandate before it hurts our business...We believe people are more important than the bottom line and that honoring God is more important than turning a profit...
>
> The government is forcing us to choose between following our faith and following the law. I say that's a choice no American and no American business should have to make...[97]

In the same letter, Mr. Green states that the government proposes to issue $1.3 million per day in fines if they refuse to comply. Even the Catholic Church is under a similar attack for exactly the same thing. Can you imagine our nation's founders turning over in their graves as this flagrant attack on our First Amendment rights continues?

In 2012, the fast-food chain Chick-fil-A was in the news because of an article published in the *Baptist Press* that quoted Dan Cathy, president of the company. While the actual quote was never really emphasized, Dan Cathy and Chick-fil-A were trashed from coast to coast by the mainstream media as being owned by some sort of intolerant, homophobic, racist monster, and liberal news organizations and celebrities lined up calling for boycotts. It was reported that the situation even led to the mayors of several cities supporting blocking construction of Chick-fil-A restaurants. What vile, hateful things did Mr. Cathy say? The truth of the matter is, not many people even bothered to check; rather, they just got on board the public lynching already underway. It is likely the majority of Americans on the lynch-mob bandwagon did not know what they were protesting. What did Dan Cathy say that was so vile?

> We are very much supportive of the family—the biblical definition of the family unit. We are a family-owned business, a family-led business, and we are married to our first wives. We give God thanks for that.[98]

Do you believe this quote was worthy of all the press that he and his company received over the following weeks and months? Despite all that you read and heard about the incident and the hate speech Mr. Cathy was reported to have said, his words were not the vile, vicious rhetoric the media tried to portray. The media appeared to intentionally avoid the actual quotation in their attempt to sensationalize the event. Please take a look at the quotation in the context of the entire article, and you will likely be even more appalled. The man said absolutely nothing offensive or disrespectful to the homosexual community. He even went as far as to say, "We don't claim to be a Christian business." He simply responded to a question (by the *Baptist Press*) about his beliefs and provided a very succinct answer. It was the media that took his comments out of context as a means of trying to discredit Christian values. If you cannot see this as an obvious attempt by Satan to try to silence Christians, then you are being blinded by his influence.

There have been several other stories in the news recently about Christian business owners being sued because they declined to take part in homosexual wedding (civil union) ceremonies (e.g., provide flower arrangements, take photographs, and bake wedding cakes). In each of these instances, the government has ruled the owners were discriminating and could not refuse the business. This trend is notable from several points of view. First, can you imagine forcing someone to participate in your ceremony that did not want to do so?

There are plenty of businesses available that would provide these services, so why would you force anyone to participate who clearly did not have his or her heart in it? Suppose the situation were reversed, and a Christian couple asked a homosexual, Muslim, or atheist to take pictures for their wedding and the photographer refused based on religious convictions. Do you think for a moment the couple would be offended and file a discrimination lawsuit? Like any reasonable person, they would simply move on to the next photographer until they found the right provider to suit their needs. This is no different than someone refusing to take a job because they do not feel comfortable in that particular situation.

Secondly, imagine if you will, the Christian photographer has been sued and forced to take pictures at a homosexual union. What if the clients decided that the Christian photographer really did not do a good enough job? You know this is coming, right? Of course, they can still claim it was caused by the same alleged discrimination. Here comes lawsuit number two against the Christian business owner. Who gets to decide how good is good enough?

Next, homosexuality is contrary to every major religion in the world today. Why do you suppose that only Christians are being singled out in this type of attack? Do you think there is the slightest possibility a Muslim baker or photographer would participate in a homosexual union? Do you think there is the slightest possibility a homosexual couple would be interested in forcing a Muslim business owner to participate in the ceremony? You might ask why not, but the answer is already obvious.

On the contrary, there are numerous anecdotal examples of Muslim business owners that have refused to do business with individuals because of their religious beliefs, yet they are allowed to continue unabated. As a matter of fact, there were videos posted on YouTube recently where a person went to several Muslim bakers to ask for a cake for a homosexual union. Of course the bakers refused, but they were not sued nor did they even make the news. Why? There is only one logical explanation.

†††

A term, *dhimmitude*, describes the legal and social conditions of Jews and Christians subject to Islamic rule. According to dhimmitude.org,[99]

> vanquished non-Muslims peoples are granted security for their life and possessions, as well as a relative self-autonomous administration and limited religious rights according to the modalities of the conquest. These rights are subject to two conditions: the payment of a poll tax (the jizya) and submission to the provisions of Islamic law...

In essence, dhimmitude means that non-Muslims are allowed to exist under Muslim rule subject to a separate set of laws. They do not have the same freedoms and responsibilities as Muslims, which manifests itself in the form of higher taxes and fewer rights. This principle of dhimmitude is being manifested against Christians in the examples noted above. If you stand up for your beliefs, you will be fined or sued into submission. Is this what America represents?

Pluralism

> He has made everything beautiful in its time. Also He has put eternity in their hearts, except that no one can find out the work that God does from beginning to end. (Eccles. 3:11)

> Jesus said to him, "I am the way, the truth, and the life. No one comes to the Father except through Me." (John 14:6)

God obviously put a natural curiosity in most people to instinctively know that there must be something more to life than just existence from day to day, and there is more to the universe than a random meeting of particles that accidentally came together to eventually form life as we know it. As a matter of fact, more than 80 percent[100] of people worldwide believe in a deity of some sort. With that being so, how could Satan address this curiosity and keep people from discovering the real God? The answer is simple: Convince people there are other gods and more than one way to heaven. Just so it's clear, the Bible explicitly states there is only one God and only one way to heaven, so if there is more than one way, then the Bible is wrong.

†††

> Then many false prophets will rise up and deceive many. And because lawlessness will abound, the love of many will grow cold. (Matt. 24:11–12)

> Now I plead with you, brethren, by the name of our Lord Jesus Christ, that you all speak the same thing, and that there be no divisions among you, but that you be perfectly joined together in the same mind and in the same judgment. (1 Cor. 1:10)

There are a number of major religions in the world today, including Christianity, Judaism, Islam, Buddhism, Hinduism, and so on. Even within the religions that refer to themselves as Christian, there are countless divisions, including but not limited to Protestants, Catholics, and Mormons. While the research for this book does not include an in-depth study of world religions, there are some people that suggest they all are similar in nature and rely on one god and advocate peace and harmony. Some even suggest that as long as you believe in one or the other, they are all good. There are still others that suggest the gods of the other religions are the same as the God of the Bible, and as long as you believe in a god, you are in.

Well, bring in the god of your choice. The Bible has many stories detailing the tendency for people to try to shape gods to fit their own personal beliefs and preferences. Even when God's people experienced His power firsthand and saw His miracles as told in the stories of Genesis and Exodus, many people still turned to worship other gods. How easy it is for Satan to divert the attention of the multitudes by creating other so-called paths to heaven. Just imagine the ability to pick the religion of your choice. If you don't like this one, then try one of the others. Just pick the one closest to your own personal values. On second thought, if they don't conform to your wishes, then modify one so that it does. Or even better yet, create your own religion (aka cult).

With the exception of Christianity, they may actually all be basically the same. Let's see if we can guess. They teach that your destiny is dependent on your actions in this world; hence, the better person you are, the more likely you are to earn a ticket to heaven. If that is so, how good do you have to be? How do you define *good*? What is the magic formula? How can you guarantee your acceptance into heaven? Are there certain acts, such as martyrdom, that will guarantee your place in heaven? (Are those acts of martyrdom targeted against Christians by any chance? i.e., Antichrist). And if there are actions that result in your access to heaven, are there certain acts that will guarantee you to be denied (i.e., grave sins)? If a person has committed a grave sin, does it preclude him or her from reaching heaven? If so, is there any point in trying to be good if your fate has already been sealed? Do you see the problem here? Christianity offers the only guaranteed way to heaven, and you don't have to worry whether or not your actions in this world are worthy.

> For the time will come when they will not endure sound doctrine, but according to their own desires, because they have itching ears, they will heap up for themselves teachers; and they will turn their ears away from the truth, and be turned aside to fables. (2 Tim. 4:3-4)

So why not create your own utopian belief and share it with the world? L. Ron Hubbard, a science-fiction writer in the twentieth century, did exactly that with his creation of Scientology. According to the scientology.org[101] website:

> Developed by L. Ron Hubbard, Scientology is a religion that offers a precise path leading to a complete and certain understanding of one's true spiritual nature and one's relationship to self, family, groups, Mankind, all life forms, the material universe, the spiritual universe and the Supreme Being.
>
> Scientology addresses the spirit—not the body or mind—and believes that Man is far more than a product of his environment, or his genes.
>
> Scientology comprises a body of knowledge which extends from certain fundamental truths. Prime among these are:
>
> Man is an immortal spiritual being.
>
> His experience extends well beyond a single lifetime.

> His capabilities are unlimited, even if not presently realized.
>
> Scientology further holds Man to be basically good, and that his spiritual salvation depends upon himself, his fellows and his attainment of brotherhood with the universe.
>
> Scientology is not a dogmatic religion in which one is asked to accept anything on faith alone. On the contrary, one discovers for oneself that the principles of Scientology are true by applying its principles and observing or experiencing the results.
>
> The ultimate goal of Scientology is true spiritual enlightenment and freedom for all...

The Scientology doctrine recognizes that humans are far more than the product of their environment and that *"Man is an immortal spiritual being."* As such, Scientology is preying on its prospective members' desire to find the meaning of life but in actuality leads you away from the Truth and apparently your money. Where was Scientology originated? Where did they get their beliefs? Does Scientology have a god? According to their website, the answer to the latter question is "most definitely." However, "Unlike religions with Judeo-Christian origins, the Church of Scientology has no set dogma concerning god that it imposes on its members." (Note their reference to the Judeo-Christian God.)

Despite its lack of credentials, Scientology is currently thriving and claims to be a religious organization. Notice how they dispel some of the most basic Christian tenets. Instead of relying on faith, Scientology doctrine says you can experience everything you need. Christianity teaches us that everyone is a sinner, but Scientology teaches that people are basically good and spiritual salvation is dependent upon oneself. It is no accident that these are flagrant attacks on basic Christian beliefs. Take a look for yourself and tour their website and see how much of their belief system is anti-Christian. As a matter of fact, compare their beliefs to the nine satanic statements of the Church of Satan noted in an earlier chapter.

> I marvel that you are turning away so soon from Him who called you in the grace of Christ, to a different gospel, which is not another; but there are some who trouble you and want to pervert the gospel of Christ. But even if we, or an angel from heaven, preach any other gospel to you than what we have preached to you, let him be accursed. As we have said before, so now I say again, if anyone preaches any other gospel to you than what you have received, let him be accursed. (Gal. 1:6–9)

A few years ago, a Mormon meetinghouse (ward) was being constructed in our neighborhood, and our church leadership decided to have a series of sermons and seminars on Mormonism to let our members know more about them and their beliefs. My initial response was complete and total apathy. I knew nothing about Mormonism, and since they called themselves the Church of Jesus Christ of Latter-Day Saints, I thought, well, they are a Protestant religion that believes in Jesus Christ, so what could be the problem? I couldn't care less about the Mormons' governmental body or rituals. As it turned out, some of the Mormon congregation got wind of our church's intent on having these seminars and were apparently quite offended by the prospect, even though they had no idea what would be said or taught. If there had not been such a stir, I probably would not have attended those seminars. In the process, I learned quite a bit about their beliefs, which resulted in a desire to learn even more, which incidentally taught me a lot about Christianity.

In actuality, the Mormon origins are not that dissimilar from those of Scientology. Mormonism started as the result of a man in the mid-nineteenth century named Joseph Smith. According to Mormon history/legend, Joseph Smith was given divine insight into how man had perverted God's message over time and that all exiting Christianity was an abomination. Through this would-be prophet, true Christianity was supposedly revealed to Joseph Smith via engravings on gold plates, which by the way, have only been reported to have been seen by close relatives and acquaintances of Joseph Smith. Since the gold plates were engraved in an unknown language, Joseph Smith had to interpret the writings by using "seer stones" that he placed in his hat to translate (although it was never explained why the gold plates were necessary if the stones provided translation).

According to Mormon legend, Native Americans (American Indians) are descendants of Israel (from prior to the tower of Babel) who made their way to the New World. To make a long story short, modern DNA testing actually proves beyond a shadow of a doubt that Native Americans are not direct descendants of Israel. Further, Joseph Smith's interpretations of other engravings (which didn't mysteriously disappear) have been discovered to be totally wrong. If he was a prophet from God, what are the chances he could have gotten it wrong? Despite the scientific evidence disproving Mormon legend, Mormonism has survived and is still flourishing today.

> Go therefore and make disciples of all the nations, baptizing them in the name of the Father and of the Son and of the Holy Spirit, teaching them to observe all things that I have commanded you; and lo, I am with you always, even to the end of the age. Amen. (Matt. 28:18–20)

The biggest and most important misinterpretations in Mormon theology are their belief that Jesus and God are two separate beings and Satan and Jesus are "spirit brothers." To boil this down into today's terms, the only road that leads to God is the True Jesus Christ. If the Mormons have chosen a different road but called it Jesus, it is still a different road and, hence, does not lead to God.

I would like to point out that I know several Mormons and have very good friends and neighbors that adhere to that faith. All the Mormons I have met have been very upstanding people, and while their theology is incorrect, at least they have biblical values. Further, in talking with some of those people, it appears that many do not know what the true Mormon faith actually represents. But to give credit where credit is due, there are a lot of Christians that don't know a lot of details about their own beliefs either. As a matter of fact, it wasn't until I studied Mormonism that I actually understood that God the Father, Jesus the Son, and the Holy Spirit are all God.

Next, consider all the Muslim countries in the world today. Unlike the United States, most of those cultures have their religion and their system of government fundamentally intertwined, so much so that their governments are actually based on Muslim theology. That means it is almost impossible to live, work, go to school, or even exist without being influenced in some way and having to acknowledge Allah. Many people who grow up in Muslim families and cultures are not given the freedom to even consider anything else. Failure to acknowledge and live according to the approved theology can and often does result in punishment, including injury or even death. Interestingly enough, many of the victims of this persecution happen to be other Muslims because their beliefs do not conform to the state-approved position. (Understand the First Amendment a little better now?)

> Beware of false prophets, who come to you in sheep's clothing, but inwardly they are ravenous wolves. You will know them by their fruits. Do men gather grapes from thornbushes or figs from thistles? (Matt. 7:15–16)

Are all churches that claim to live by the Bible true paths to God? Is claiming that you believe in Jesus Christ alone sufficient to ensure your salvation? The answer is an unequivocal no. The Christian church is marred with numerous instances of dark times where people committed atrocities in the name of God. From the Spanish Inquisition to the Salem witch trials, there have been some notable problems with Christianity, and detractors will try to use those events as evidence supporting the destructiveness of religion on human existence. This is a brilliant strategy to get God out of the picture; however, do not fall into the trap of trying to defend your faith as being connected with these abominations. There are no biblical references to suggest Christians should put nonbelievers to death. The Bible clearly states that we should not judge one another, and in fact, we are specifically commanded to love our enemies.

> For such are false apostles, deceitful workers, transforming themselves into apostles of Christ. And no wonder! For Satan himself transforms himself into an angel of light. Therefore it is no great thing if his ministers also transform themselves into ministers of righteousness, whose end will be according to their works. (2 Cor. 11:13–15)

Many of you may not be old enough to remember James Warren Jones (Jim Jones), the leader of the Peoples Temple. Jim Jones served as pastor at several churches in the United States until he finally decided to move his congregation to Guyana to further his communistic beliefs. His dictatorship-type control led to abuses and eventually dissent among his congregation. This dissent led to a congressional investigation that eventually caused him to implode. In 1978, Jim Jones ordered a mass suicide among his congregation, which also resulted in the murder of a US congressman and four members of his delegation. Jim Jones's story is significant and worth investigating just to see how twisted this man really was. Is there anybody alive that would not agree this man was possessed by evil? The stories of this insane preacher would be effective in scaring anybody away from religion.

Let's fast-forward to the 1990s and Vernon Wayne Howell, who later changed his name to David Koresh. David Koresh was a self-proclaimed prophet and leader of a religious sect called the Branch Davidians near Waco, Texas. Similar to the Jim Jones story, his narcissistic attitude eventually led to his demise when his compound was burned to the ground after a raid by the FBI and ATF. David Koresh and fifty-four other adults and twenty-eight children died in that fire on April 19, 1993. While the government's methods were questionable, there was absolutely no reason for this tragedy other than the selfish motives of a deranged man. Again, is there any doubt that this man was also possessed by evil?

As previously stated, if there is more than one path to God, then the Bible is false. The Bible clearly states there is only one God and one Way to reach

Him, and that is through a relationship with the True Jesus Christ. Whether you believe in a different god or a different Jesus, these are all paths to destruction that are all well-conceived distractions created by the great deceiver himself. For those who hear God's voice calling, Satan is providing counterfeit paths. Whether knowingly or not, the creators/proponents of these religions/cults are accomplices in furthering Satan's agenda.

An Evil System of Government

In the creation-versus-evolution debate, Bill Nye claimed numerous times that science can be used to make predictions about our world and that the Bible cannot. To the contrary, a major theme of this book is to point out that we can make predictions about Satan's agenda and influence to explain the utter nonsense and insanity that are occurring in our culture as well as cultures around the world, which brings us to the next point. Would you believe in Satan (and therefore God) if we could accurately predict Satan's agenda, goals, and influence? If several dozen predictions about Satan's future influence were laid out and they started to come to fruition, how many would it take before you opened your eyes to the truth and did something about it? After all, this is following Bill Nye's argument that true science can be used to make predictions about our future. Well, hold on, because we have saved the best evidence for last. If you have an open mind, consider this partial list of goals:

13. Do away with all loyalty oaths.
15. Capture one or both of the political parties in the United States.
16. Use technical decisions of the courts to weaken basic American institutions by claiming their activities violate civil rights.
17. Get control of the schools. Use them as transmission belts for socialism and current communist propaganda. Soften the curriculum. Get control of teachers' associations. Put the party line in textbooks.
21. Gain control of key positions in radio, TV, and motion pictures.

22. Continue discrediting American culture by degrading all forms of artistic expression. An American Communist cell was told to "eliminate all good sculpture from parks and buildings, substitute shapeless, awkward and meaningless forms."
23. Control art critics and directors of art museums. "Our plan is to promote ugliness, repulsive, meaningless art."
24. Eliminate all laws governing obscenity by calling them "censorship" and a violation of free speech and free press.
25. Break down cultural standards of morality by promoting pornography and obscenity in books, magazines, motion pictures, radio, and TV.
26. Present homosexuality, degeneracy, and promiscuity as "normal, natural, healthy."
27. Infiltrate the churches and replace revealed religion with "social" religion. Discredit the Bible and emphasize the need for intellectual maturity, which does not need a "religious crutch."
28. Eliminate prayer or any phase of religious expression in the schools on the grounds that it violates the principle of "separation of church and state."
29. Discredit the American Constitution by calling it inadequate, old-fashioned, out of step with modern needs, and a hindrance to cooperation between nations on a worldwide basis.
32. Support any socialist movement to give centralized control over any part of the culture—education, social agencies, welfare programs, mental health clinics, and so on.
36. Infiltrate and gain control of more unions.
40. Discredit the family as an institution. Encourage promiscuity and easy divorce.
41. Emphasize the need to raise children away from the negative influence of parents. Attribute prejudices, mental blocks, and retarding of children to the suppressive influence of parents.
42. Create the impression that violence and insurrection are legitimate aspects of the American tradition, and that students and special-interest groups should rise up and use "united force" to solve economic, political, or social problems.

If you think this is an unfair test because most of these have already come true, you are correct about them being true, but it is indeed a fair test. The reason is because these goals are a portion of the list of forty-five goals of the Communist Party that were published more than fifty years ago in a book called *The Naked Communist*[102] (pp. 266–296) by Cleon Skousen, a former FBI agent.

> "We must combat religion—this is the ABC of materialism, and consequently of Marxism."
>
> —Nikolai Lenin (*The Naked Communist*, p. 37)

Try to imagine what form of government would serve Satan's interests the most effectively. One could argue that getting people to kill others in the name of god is a pretty effective means to spread evil. Imagine teaching adherents it was their duty to create havoc, murder, maim, and destroy, all in the name of god. The news is full of stories of Islamic extremists committing all sorts of atrocities in the name of their religion, many targeting Christians, including women and children. But then again, religion is basically a set of beliefs (or rules), and Satan does not go by the rules. Satan wants absolute power to control our lives and does not want peace and harmony. With that said, think about what form of government would best serve his agenda. The following are the four major premises of Communism as written by Cleon Skousen in *The Naked Communist*:

- "Everything in existence came about as a result of ceaseless motion among the forces of nature" (*The Naked Communist*, p. 362).
- "Human beings are only graduate beasts" (*The Naked Communist*, p. 363).
- "There is no such thing as innate right or wrong" (*The Naked Communist*, p. 364).
- "That all religion must be overthrown because it inhibits the spirit of the world revolution" (*The Naked Communist*, p. 364).

Do any of these statements sound familiar? If not, please refer back to the nine satanic statements of the Church of Satan. (Keep in mind

The Naked Communist was published long before the founding of the Church of Satan.) Further, Karl Marx, the founder of communism, wrote in his doctoral dissertation: "In one word—I hate all the gods!" (*The Naked Communist,* p. 12).

> When Karl Marx was asked what his object in life was, he said, "My object in life is to dethrone God and destroy capitalism." (*The Naked Communist,* p. 37)

Likewise, Anantole Lunarcharsky, former Russian Commissioner of Education, alleged:

> We hate Christians and Christianity. Even the best of them must be considered our worst enemies. They preach love of one's neighbor and mercy, which is contrary to our principles. Christian love is an obstacle to the development of the Revolution. Down with love of our neighbor! What we want is hate...Only then can we conquer the universe. (*The Naked Communist,* p. 73)

Did you know that communist founders believe "atheism is a natural and inseparable part of Marxism" and that it is imperative to not only ignore religion but replace it with "militant atheism" (*The Naked Communist,* p. 365)? In other words, atheism is absolutely essential to communism.

> The communist believes the only morals are that which is in the interest of the class struggle. If it helps, then it is good, if not, it is bad. In other words, "the end justifies the means." (*The Naked Communist,* p. 38)

> "We therefore reject every attempt to impose on us any moral dogma whatever..."
>
> —Friedrich Engle, *Handbook of Marxism,* p. 249 (*The Naked Communist,* p. 310)

The main reason atheism is such an integral part of communism is because there can be absolutely no morals in that belief system. Whatever or whoever does not agree to the party line must be eliminated with extreme prejudice. It is also likely his or her family and friends would be eliminated as well. This is because communists have no respect for human life. If they did, then killing their opponents would be murder rather than political expedience. Further, communists truly believe in survival of the fittest. If you are not a productive member of the collective, then you are eliminated…with extreme prejudice. If you are too old or have a physical or mental impairment that is a detriment to the communist machine, you are eliminated…with extreme prejudice. This belief would indeed put us on the same level as other beasts of nature. Under communism, killing would be just a natural part of our survival and our way of life.

Atheism is also essential because the communist party (Satan) does not want loyalties to anything or anyone other than the communist party. Anything that could elicit devotion away from Satan and his agenda must be eliminated. There is no right or wrong; there is only that which is good for the party because with communism (as with Satan), the ends justify the means.

Any student of history should know that communism has not only failed but has been a catastrophic failure every time it has been tried. There are countless examples of mass genocide where millions of people have been killed for the good of the communist party. Wikipedia.org chronicles a book called *The Black Book of Communism*[103] and states:

> In the introduction, editor Stéphane Courtois states that "Communist regimes…turned mass crime into a full-blown system of government." He claims that a death toll totals 94 million. The breakdown of the number of deaths given by Courtois is as follows:
>
> - 65 million in the People's Republic of China
> - 20 million in the Soviet Union
> - 2 million in Cambodia
> - 2 million in North Korea

- 1.7 million in Africa
- 1.5 million in Afghanistan
- 1 million in the Communist states of Eastern Europe
- 1 million in Vietnam
- 150,000 in Latin America (mainly Cuba)
- 10,000 deaths "resulting from actions of the international Communist movement and Communist parties not in power..."

> Courtois claims that communist regimes are responsible for a greater number of deaths than any other political ideal or movement, including Nazism. The statistics of victims include executions, famine, deaths resulting from deportations, physical confinement, or through forced labor.

If communism has never worked and has a well-documented history of death and destruction, why would anyone support and advocate this system of government? In order to appreciate the threat of communism and the relationship to Satan, you must understand the basic tenets of communism. The author of *The Naked Communist* points out that Karl Marx and Friedrich Engles "announced to mankind that the new program of International Communism stood for: 1) the overthrow of capitalism, 2) the abolition of private property, 3) the elimination of the family as a social unity, 4) the abolition of all classes, 5) the overthrow of all governments, 6) the establishment of a communist order with a communal ownership of property in a classless, stateless society" (*The Naked Communist*, p. 17).

Communists have the goal and believe it is their duty to take over the world. They have no intention of coexisting. This would be a good place to provide some modern and historical documentation for the encroachment of socialism/communism, but the previous chapters have already covered that quite thoroughly. It is worth noting that the previous chapters were written long before coming across this information on communism. As we examine more and more of the evidence, all the pieces start fitting very nicely together once we understand the problem.

If there is an ongoing attempt to move America into communism, what would be the best way to do that? Let's see, communism seeks to destroy capitalism and eliminate private property. How about destroying its currency by bankrupting the country? How about redistributing wealth by taking from the industrious and giving to an ever-growing dependent entitlement class? How about destroying religion and eliminating all morals? Remember, this list was published more than fifty years ago. Recall Bill Nye's useful science predictions. Well, this is the science of evil. We knew their goals and agenda and predicted its coming, but unfortunately most of us sit idly by as our freedoms are being eroded away. How can a rational freedom-loving American (whether Christian, agnostic, or atheist) not be chilled to the bone about how far this agenda has progressed?

> "Each will produce according to his ability and each will receive according to his need." (*The Naked Communist*, p. 59)

> It seems the phantom of the Communist hope can only arise from the bowels of the earth through the ashes of all that now is. Communism must be built for one purpose—to destroy. (*The Naked Communist*, p. 89)

Expect proponents of communism to use an incremental and systematic approach to try to corrupt and conquer. They have been effectively working behind the scenes to corrupt our way of life for decades, and they will get louder and bolder as they promote this evil system of government. As a matter of fact, the Revolutionary Communist Party has recently come out of the closet and taken advantage of the recent protests involving police shootings in Ferguson, Missouri, and New York, New York. (Yes, there is a Communist Party in the United States.) Please notice some of the protestors' signs have referenced their website (www.revcom.us). Why would anyone go down a path that is certain to fail? There is only one logical explanation. If you are still not convinced, please take the time to watch the movie *Agenda: Grinding America Down*.[104] It provides a very informative analysis of ties between communism and many of our past and current leaders. This is the resource that led to my discovery of the book *The Naked Communist.*

As our culture progresses, be on the lookout for the telltale signs of the encroachment of communism, including:

- the ends justify the means;
- references to revolution;
- divisive class warfare;
- lack of fiscal responsibility and/or even the acknowledgment of the problem;
- erosion of morals (promiscuity, abortion, sanctity of life, and so on);
- references to economic justice or social justice (code words for socialism);
- incremental erosion of our basic rights;
- more control over our lives by the state, with particular emphasis on the youth with less control by families; and
- change in focus from patriotism to a worldview.

WATCHMAN ON THE WALL

> And a servant of the Lord must not quarrel but be gentle to all, able to teach, patient, in humility correcting those who are in opposition, if God perhaps will grant them repentance, so that they may know the truth, and that they may come to their senses and escape the snare of the devil, having been taken captive by him to do his will. (2 Tim. 2:24–26)

THE FOLLOWING IS a little more detail on what this text has referred to as the homosexual lobby and their agenda. Just as a reminder, Christians are commanded by the Bible to love the sinner and hate the sin. There is nothing in the Bible or this book that suggests Christians should be hateful or intolerant of anybody at any time. As a matter of fact, we are specifically warned about judging our neighbor because we are all sinful. With that said, let's take a look at the true agenda of the homosexual lobby. I was almost through writing this book when I inadvertently came across an article called the "Homosexual Manifesto,"[105] written by Michael Swift and published in 1987, along with a few other articles, including "The Overhauling of Straight America"[106] by Marshall Kirk and Erastes Pill, "The 1972 Gay Rights Platform" created at the National Coalition of Gay Organizations Convention held in Chicago in 1972, and "Platform of the 1993 March on Washington for Lesbian, Gay, and Bi Equal Rights and Liberation." These documents clearly convey what was already perfectly obvious about the homosexual agenda, specifically, a systematic and graduated plan to manipulate and indoctrinate the public into accepting the homosexual lifestyle as mainstream.

The article "The Overhauling of Straight America" has been described as the "blueprint for transforming the social values of straight America." This 1987 article outlines the homosexual lobby's strategy and tactics with bold frankness which is clearly evident in our current culture. The article clearly exposes how we are being duped and being manipulated into changing our culture into something the vast majority of us do not believe. The following are select quotes from the article. Remember, this article was published almost three decades ago.

> [1] TALK ABOUT GAYS AND GAYNESS AS LOUDLY AND AS OFTEN AS POSSIBLE
>
> The principle behind this advice is simple: almost any behavior begins to look normal if you are exposed to enough of it at close quarters and among your acquaintances...
>
> The way to benumb raw sensitivities about homosexuality is to have a lot of people talk about the subject in a neutral or supportive way. Open and frank talk makes the subject seem less furtive, alien, and sinful, more above-board...
>
> The average American household watches over seven hours of TV daily. Those hours open up a gateway into the private world of straights, through which a Trojan horse might be passed...
>
> So far, gay Hollywood has provided our best covert weapon in the battle to desensitize the mainstream. Bit by bit over the past ten years, gay characters and gay themes have been introduced into TV programs and films (though often this has been done to achieve comedic and ridiculous affects)...
>
> When conservative churches condemn gays, there are only two things we can do to confound the homophobia of true believers. First, we can use talk to muddy the moral waters. This means publicizing support for gays by more moderate churches, raising theological objections

> of our own about conservative interpretations of biblical teachings, and exposing hatred and inconsistency. Second, we can undermine the moral authority of homophobic churches by portraying them as antiquated backwaters, badly out of step with the times and with the latest findings of psychology. Against the mighty pull of institutional Religion one must set the mightier draw of Science & Public Opinion (the shield and sword of that accursed "secular humanism"). Such an unholy alliance has worked well against churches before, on such topics as divorce and abortion. With enough open talk about the prevalence and acceptability of homosexuality, that alliance can work again here.

Think about all of the airtime that the media outlets have given to this minute sector of our population. Why is there such a huge homosexual presence in the media today?

> [2] PORTRAY GAYS AS VICTIMS, NOT AS AGGRESSIVE CHALLENGERS
>
> In any campaign to win over the public, gays must be cast as victims in need of protection so that straights will be inclined by reflex to assume the role of protector...
>
> First, the mainstream should be told that gays are victims of fate, in the sense that most never had a choice to accept or reject their sexual preference. The message must read: "As far as gays can tell, they were born gay, just as you were born heterosexual or white or black or bright or athletic. Nobody ever tricked or seduced them; they never made a choice, and are not morally blameworthy. What they do isn't willfully contrary—it's only natural for them. This twist of fate could as easily have happened to you..."

While homosexuals may have been persecuted in years past, this is certainly not the case in America today. This is nothing more than a pathetic attempt to manipulate public opinion. On the contrary, if anything, Christians are now the victims in today's politically correct society.

> [3] GIVE PROTECTORS A JUST CAUSE
>
> Our campaign should not demand direct support for homosexual practices, should instead take antidiscrimination as its theme…
>
> The homophobes clothe their emotional revulsion in the daunting robes of religious dogma, so defenders of gay rights must be ready to counter dogma with principle…

This strategy has been clearly exposed in the previous chapters, particularly when it compromises the rights of Christians.

> [4] MAKE GAYS LOOK GOOD
>
> In order to make a Gay Victim sympathetic to straights you have to portray him as Everyman…

Examine all the TV programming and how it portrays homosexuals and how that image has progressed over time. Again, why is there such a huge homosexual presence in the media today?

> [5] MAKE THE VICTIMIZERS LOOK BAD
>
> At a later stage of the media campaign for gay rights—long after other gay ads have become commonplace—it will be time to get tough with remaining opponents. To be blunt, they must be vilified…Our goal here is twofold. First, we seek to replace the mainstream's self-righteous pride about its homophobia with shame and guilt. Second, we intend to make the antigays look so nasty that average Americans will want to dissociate themselves from such types…
>
> The public should be shown images of ranting homophobes whose secondary traits and beliefs disgust middle America…

The propaganda ministry goes out of the way to portray Christians in the negative. This has been clearly demonstrated in the examples cited in this text. Again, why attack Christianity for this perceived plight?

> [6] SOLICIT FUNDS: THE BUCK STOPS HERE
>
> Any massive campaign of this kind would require unprecedented expenditures for months or even years—an unprecedented fundraising drive…
>
> [7] GETTING ON THE AIR, OR, YOU CAN'T GET THERE FROM HERE
>
> Without access to TV, radio, and the mainstream press, there will be no campaign…
>
> Because most straightforward appeals are impossible, the National Gay Task Force has had to cultivate quiet backroom liaisons with broadcast companies and newsrooms…

IMDB.com lists 143[107] gay-themed TV series, and Wikipedia.org[108] even lists numerous animated series with homosexual characters. Do you really believe this emphasis in programming is representative of America?

With the strategy and tactics so clearly exposed almost three decades ago, how is it possible that we have allowed this deception? This is no accident but a clearly orchestrated effort to erode the morals of our nation and trash traditional Christian values. These documents provide undisputable proof of the homosexual lobby's agenda and tactics, and they are not even trying to hide them. It should also be noted that the Communist Party's strategy of destroying morality includes promoting a similar homosexual agenda.

> So you, son of man: I have made you a watchman for the house of Israel; therefore you shall hear a word from My mouth and warn them for Me. When I say to the wicked, 'O wicked man, you shall surely die!' and you do not speak to warn the wicked from his way, that wicked man shall die in his iniquity; but his blood I will require at your hand. Nevertheless if you warn the wicked to turn from his way,

> and he does not turn from his way, he shall die in his iniquity; but you have delivered your soul.
>
> Therefore you, O son of man, say to the house of Israel: 'Thus you say, "If our transgressions and our sins lie upon us, and we pine away in them, how can we then live?" Say to them: 'As I live,' says the Lord God, 'I have no pleasure in the death of the wicked, but that the wicked turn from his way and live. Turn, turn from your evil ways! For why should you die, O house of Israel?' (Ezek. 33:7–11)

Christians are not homophobic, racist, or hateful for proclaiming the gospel. As a matter of fact, they are acting out of love in doing so. To do otherwise would indeed be a sign of indifference and lack of love. Why do you think Christians are willing to put up with all of the hate, prejudice, and persecution for standing up for what the Bible says? Why do you think they are willing to even lose their jobs and places of business for this cause? As Christians, we are commanded to share the Word. What you do with that Word is up to you. Don't try to mischaracterize Christians as hateful because they love you enough to tell the Truth. If you disagree with the Christian view, just say, "Thank you; I love you too."

THE DATA

NOW LET'S EXAMINE the evidence and compare it with what we know about Satan and his character to see if there is confirmation of his presence and influence.

Based on our hypothesis, we expect Satan to attempt to undermine the sovereignty of God, which includes trying to convince us that there is no God. How else can you explain the militant anti-Christian movement dedicated to a belief in a nonbelief, atheism? Why are the vast majority of these groups specifically targeting Christianity and not other religions? This anti-Christian sentiment was predicted thousands of years ago and is well chronicled in the Bible and confirmed day after day as our culture continues down this dark path. When have you ever heard of an atheist group claiming there is no Mohammed or Allah or Buddha or some other god? But of course, what would be the point? With fewer than 10 percent of people worldwide who identify themselves as atheist, how else can you explain the systematic effort to eliminate religious expression in our culture?

Why is evolution so emphatically taught as fact when it is really only a theory? Why does the science establishment try to eliminate any evidence contrary to this theory, even to the point of preventing any discussion of it? Why are scientists so hostile toward the concept of intelligent design? Why do atheists insist that God and science cannot coexist? What other possible explanation can there be? The previous chapters chronicle numerous examples of how the politically correct science establishment suggests there is a conflict between the Bible and science. As noted, God wrote the laws of physics, so there is absolutely no reason why the Bible should conflict with true science. Science and religion are not mutually exclusive, and to suggest otherwise is an insincere attempt at keeping people from finding out on their own.

The evidence of Satan's attempts to convince us that God does not exist and atheists' hostility toward Christianity provides undisputable support for our hypothesis.

Based on our hypothesis, our expectation is that Satan will attempt to portray Christians and Christianity in a bad light and sensationalize anything that can reflect negatively on it. The examples of self-proclaimed Christian churches, including Westboro Baptist Church, the Branch Davidians (David Koresh), and the Peoples Temple (Jim Jones), would frighten any sane person away from religion. To suggest these examples are somehow representative of Christianity is beyond absurd because there is no Scripture to support these abominations. The evidence of Satan's attacks on Christians, the church, and the gospel is overwhelming, which provides further support of our hypothesis.

Based on our hypothesis, our expectation is that Satan will attempt to provide false pathways to God. These types of temptations are clearly chronicled and predicted in the Bible. While many religions have existed for thousands of years, others have only recently come into being and cater to just about any belief, including some that were founded as late as the nineteenth and twentieth centuries. Doesn't it make sense that if there is an all-knowing God of the universe, He would make Himself known to His people? Whether the earth is ten thousand or ten billion years old, does it make any sense that God would wait until the last one hundred to one hundred fifty years to reveal Himself? All of these false religions are an effective means of keeping many people from discovering the real God and in many cases very effective at helping persecute Christians. And not only does Satan provide counterfeit paths to God and heaven, he has even gotten so bold that he is now seeking people to serve him directly through the Church of Satan. The evidence of these false pathways is overwhelming, which provides further evidence in support of our hypothesis.

Based on our hypothesis, our expectation is that Satan will attempt to destroy God's Word by any means possible. Because he cannot remove the Bible all at once, he is attempting to detract from its message in an incremental manner. The examples cited in previous chapters clearly identify numerous assaults occurring in this country that are nothing more than blatant attempts to undermine fundamental Christian values and beliefs. We have systematically given in to numerous temptations, such as overindulgence, sexual immorality, and materialism, and not only have we allowed this systematic erosion of our moral foundation; it appears we have encouraged and embraced it. In short, Satan is using temptations and, where possible, political correctness to encourage/demand an erosion of our moral foundation. In lockstep, the government is slowly and systematically encroaching on our rights of free speech and freedom of religion, all in the name of tolerance. There is tolerance for everyone and everything except Christians and traditional Christian values. The evidence of Satan's attempts at eliminating the gospel is not only obvious but overwhelming; which is some of the best and strongest evidence in support of our hypothesis. Why would anyone feel threatened by Christian values?

Based on our hypothesis, we expect Satan to attempt to discourage Christianity through any means possible in order to make Christians uncomfortable in their beliefs. Therefore, when Satan can't attack the message, he attacks the messenger. How many times have we seen this, especially in politics? Rather than debating an issue on its own merits, the opposition reverts to personally attacking their opponent. Satan knows he can't compete against the Word of God, so he resorts to personal attacks against Christians to keep them quiet. The evidence provided in the previous chapters clearly demonstrates an overwhelming and increasing prejudice against Christians. Businesses such as Chick-fil-A and Hobby Lobby are being bullied and threatened simply because the owners have Christian beliefs. Radicals are even attempting to boycott and destroy businesses with owners who express Christian values, which sends a clear message to other business owners that they need to keep their beliefs to themselves or face possible financial persecution. In a country that provides such an emphasis on equality, why is it acceptable to pick on this one segment of our society and treat Christians as second-class citizens? The examples of attacks on Christians is overwhelming and accelerating, which provides additional evidence in support of our hypothesis.

Based on our hypothesis, we expect Satan to attempt to not only downplay but deny the influence that Christianity has had on the development of our nation. The evidence of our religious cultural heritage is overwhelming and undeniable. Even if you believe our founders to be ignorant regarding their beliefs, there is no denying its existence. Why would there be an effort to eliminate the facts? The examples of the agents of Satan attempting to deny our Christian heritage clearly support our hypothesis.

Satan is also using political correctness to extract God from all aspects of public life, and his allies are attempting to use the First Amendment to the Constitution to eliminate religious expression. The very same language our founders intended to acknowledge our right to free exercise of religion is being used to destroy it. These attacks on our freedom of speech and expression provide evidence in support of our hypothesis.

Further, because the United States is a testament to the power of God, we expect Satan and his agents to try to dismantle and destroy our country by any means possible. The evidence cited in the previous chapters clearly shows incremental and increasing attacks on our culture, our financial security, and the sovereignty of our country by enemies both internal and external. Why do we continue down this path of destruction when the consequences are so dire? Why do so many people (especially our leaders) have trouble even acknowledging there is a problem? The examples of the attacks on our country and our way of life are obvious, overwhelming, and increasing, and provide further undisputable evidence in support of our hypothesis.

Reflect a moment on the evidence cited in the previous chapters and ask yourself this question: What does it take to meet the minimum requirements of a theory being accepted as scientific fact? To help demonstrate, let's briefly examine three other scientific subjects that are taught as fact.

- Science would have us believe that life on Earth was created by random chance, and through evolution of species, the diversity of life on Earth was created as it exists today.
- Science would have us believe that the earth and creation are billions of years old.
- While chemistry is a rather complex scientific field of study, it is actually worth mentioning as we ponder the evidence from our experiment regarding the existence of Satan. Specifically, let's reexamine the theories on the structure of the atom.

In the first example, evolution, what would you believe to be the level of proof that science has obtained? What level of evidence is there to support that life came from the elements through random chance and that life on Earth as we know it today evolved over billions of years from one species to another? If we acknowledge there is not an acceptable test for the existence of God, then we can make an alternative hypothesis that life came from the elements. With the fact that we are here and the fossil record supports the existence of ancient life on Earth, indeed we may have some credible evidence that life on

Earth is at least different now than it used to be. However, science has yet to create life from the elements even though science claims to understand its composition, construction, and processes. Let's say that again. Science teaches us that life began by random chance by the combining of the elements billions of years ago; nonetheless, science has never been able to create even the simplest life-form from the elements. Science further claims that all life on Earth evolved from lower forms of life, yet there is absolutely no proof whatsoever that one species has ever evolved into another, or in biblical terms, changed kinds. While we are taught that evolution is a gradual process, there is absolutely no fossil evidence to support one kind evolving into another. Darwin's observations only documented examples of adaptation, not evolution.

In short, the evolution that we are being taught as fact in classrooms all over the world today has only achieved a level of proof that couldn't convince a jury that a person had stolen a ten-cent piece of gum. If you would like to see more evidence regarding the weaknesses in the theory of evolution, please watch Ray Comfort's video entitled *Evolution vs. God: Shaking the Foundations of Faith.*[109] It is available via the Internet and provides a very enlightening analysis on how flimsy the theory of evolution really is and how people are hoodwinked into believing this theory as fact. Unlike some of the anti-Christian films, where they interview lay people, Ray Comfort actually seeks out and interviews experts in the field of evolution.

Our second example, regarding the age of the earth, is a bit more complicated. Indeed, in the absence of hard evidence to the contrary, it certainly appears that the earth is quite old. The earthly processes of plate tectonics, weather, erosion, and so on, along with time, could account for many of our observations in nature. In this case, we may have met the level of proof as having a preponderance of evidence and may even go so far as to call it clear and convincing proof. But the fact remains that science assumes the earth has a very inflated age because they cannot explain things through any other rational observable scientific theory.

Further, the theories on the age of the earth (and evolution) are based on an assumption called uniformitarianism, which is another theory that cannot be proven. With that said, did you know that the oceans are getting saltier?

If uniformitarianism holds true and the earth is truly billions of years old, then the seas would be too salty to support life. Did you know the moon's orbit is increasing by a few centimeters to a few inches per year? Again, if the earth is billions of years old, the moon would no longer be in the earth's orbit. There are countless other examples in science that call into question the true age of the earth that are contrary to the accepted theory. Keep this in mind as you ponder this question: If God created the earth for us, what would the earth look like when He finished? It would have needed to be a mature and functioning ecosystem, not just the makings for one. How many rings did the Tree of Life have in the center of the Garden of Eden on day number seven of creation? (Imagine Bill Nye in the Garden of Eden having chopped down the Tree of Life to count the tree rings in order to try to convince Adam and Eve that God was lying about the age of the earth.)

Finally, let's take a look at our third example, regarding the structure of the atom. The word *atom* came from the term *atomos*, which was first used in approximately 450 BC, intended to refer to the smallest indivisible particle of matter. The models of the atom provide a theory about its characteristics and structure, and we can now predict the behavior of atoms with great accuracy. This behavior was not discovered by looking through a microscope but by thousands of experiments to test and retest each hypothesis and then make a conclusion from the evidence. While our knowledge of chemistry suggests we have gotten it right regarding the structure of the atom, we still do not know for certain that they are 100 percent accurate representations. There are no microscopes that can physically see individual atoms. On the other hand, these empirical models are able to predict behavior of atoms with almost certain accuracy. At one time, the definition of "beyond a reasonable doubt" included "you are willing to rely and act upon without hesitation in the most important of your own affairs."[110] Let's be honest. We rely on our knowledge of chemistry every single day of our lives, which includes the most important of our affairs. For example, we rely on that knowledge to produce the chemicals and drugs we use to keep us healthy. Astronauts rely on our knowledge of chemistry to provide the fuel that propels them into space and oxygen that provides their life support. The same goes for many other professions that not only use those chemicals but the models are also used for their manufacturing. We don't produce chemicals by chance, do we? While there may be some level of uncertainty, it certainly appears that we have met the threshold of beyond a reasonable doubt. In this case, we have to get it right, or people could die. With the first two theories, evolution and age of the earth, there are no immediate worldly consequences if we get them wrong.

Our experiment on the existence of Satan is very closely in line with the chemistry example and is certainly more absolute than either of the first two theories. Nonetheless, feel free to continue to test our theory. Keep in mind that Satan is the great deceiver, so a direct test for his existence may not be possible. The microscopes are not sufficiently strong enough to see him, but we do know enough about him and his character that we can generally predict the presence of his influence with almost certain accuracy.

†††

So, have we proven the existence of Satan? The Bible speaks clearly about the evil one and clearly describes his nature. The evidence clearly supports the existence of evil and an ongoing anti-Christian crusade that is actively attacking every Christian value that a person could possibly have, including but not limited to family, marriage, sex, and abstinence. The Bible is a collection of books that was written thousands of years ago, so there is no possible way our ancestors could have possibly predicted our future without some divine inspiration. While there are some efforts to discredit other religions, they are insignificant compared to the magnitude of the anti-Christian sentiment that exists today. Further, having false religions only helps foster the notion that there is no deity, and religious sects with bad reputations can reflect negatively on Christianity through association. Just examine the evil that exists with Al Qaeda and ISIL/ISIS. If there are so many people that believe all religion is bad, why does our politically correct culture fail to call this evil what it really is?

If there is no God and no Satan, how can you possibly explain the prolific anti-Christian sentiment that exists in the United States and throughout the world today? Why is there such a concerted effort to eliminate (Christian) religious expression? Judge for yourself how America has continued to drift away from its founding principles and how our society has suffered because of it. Just open your eyes to the anti-Christian nature of our politics, our entertainment, our culture, and even our own behavior, and you will see that there is only one logical explanation.

The previous chapters have outlined example after example of anti-Christian (evil) activities and behavior, as well as exposed many of Satan's strategies that are effective at keeping people from discovering God. Individual examples, while possibly circumstantial by themselves, when combined provide evidence beyond a reasonable doubt for the existence of Satan. Not only is the evidence abundant; examples supporting our hypothesis are increasing in frequency and magnitude. Think about how our culture used to have moral absolutes and how that has evolved in recent years. Today you can be a lying, cheating, perjuring adulterer and still serve as the top public official of the United States. Today kids are allowed to decide what sex they want to represent. How can you possibly explain why the solutions our leaders continue to put in place only exacerbate the problems they were intended to solve? These are all clear examples of Satan's influence.

While there are likely to be skeptics, it is really not unexpected. If the people of the Bible can witness God's power and glory firsthand and still turn away from Him, the evidence cited here is not going to change the mind of someone who has not been touched by the Holy Spirit. Nonetheless, if you just take the time and listen for God's voice, you will find He is and has always been right beside you.

As you hear of current events and trends in our culture, compare the results with our hypothesis and ask yourself these questions, especially when things don't seem to make sense:

- Do they support any of the agenda of the Church of Satan (satanic statements)?
- Do they support the parallel anti-Christian/antimoral agenda of the Communist Party?

- Do they erode our Constitution and our God-given rights?
- Do they weaken our country?
- Do they degrade the sanctity of human life?
- Do they attack traditional family values?
- Does the proposed solution put in place to solve a problem only exacerbate the problem it was intended to solve?
- Do the proponents of these actions believe the ends justify the means (e.g., it is OK to lie in order to achieve the desired result)?
- If Satan is real, *what would he do differently*?

And finally, if indeed you become motivated to seriously investigate God and what it means to become a Christian, be prepared to counter all of the obstacles Satan tries to put in your path. As a matter of fact, be prepared to make a list to help you conduct your own experiment. Without a shadow of doubt, Satan will go to great lengths to make sure you fail, which will be proof positive of his existence.

What's Next?

> Do not fear any of those things which you are about to suffer. Indeed, the devil is about to throw some of you into prison, that you may be tested, and you will have tribulation ten days. Be faithful until death, and I will give you the crown of life. (Rev. 2:10)

We probably do not have the capacity to even imagine the deceit and treachery Satan has in store for us in the near or distant future. However, it certainly appears it will get much worse before it gets better unless we actively choose to stand up for what is right. In the meantime, here are just a few thoughts for you to take home.

The Supreme Court's decision striking down the ban on same-sex marriage (making it legal in all fifty states) will probably have the most far-reaching effect of any of Satan's advancements in the last thousand years. This decision will be used again and again to persecute Christians and destroy Christian values. For example, officials in Oregon have recently fined a baker $135,000 for refusing to bake a wedding cake for a same-sex couple. How in the world does refusing to bake a single cake equate to a fine of $135,000? The baker did not refuse to serve the customer; rather, the baker refused to make a specific cake she found offensive. What if they had asked the baker to make a cake shaped like a penis? Could the baker refuse? What is the difference? Expect the homosexual lobby to continue to seek out and specifically target Christian business owners with the intent of creating more of this type of example.

Religious institutions are currently exempt from having to endorse homosexuality and recognize same-sex unions, but it will not be long before there are attempts to eliminate this exemption as well. Why should pastors be exempt from performing homosexual ceremonies? Why should seminaries be allowed to exclude homosexuals? How would these be any different than the baker who refused to participate in a same-sex wedding? It won't be long before these examples make the news and there is a renewed effort to eliminate the religious exemption altogether. The homosexual lobby will continue attacks on Christian institutions using same-sex marriage as an instrument of destruction. These attacks will likely be used to eliminate the tax-exempt status for churches, which will further limit the ability of Christians to carry out the Great Commission.

> The very purpose of a Bill of Rights was to withdraw certain subjects from the vicissitudes of political controversy, to place them beyond the reach of majorities and officials and to establish them as legal principles to be applied by the courts. One's right to life, liberty, and property, to free speech, a free press, freedom of worship and assembly, and other fundamental rights may not be submitted to vote; they depend on the outcome of no elections.
>
> —Justice Robert H. Jackson, Opinion of the Court, June 3, 1940, in Minersville School District v. Gobitis, 310 US 586

While our current system of government does acknowledge and affirm our basic God-given rights, it is constantly under attack. In reality, our current system of government may be the only thing holding Satan in check. Therefore, expect continued attempts to implement controls on our lives for our own good and in the name of tolerance, thereby limiting religious expression, which can and will eventually expand to whatever the government deems appropriate. But in order to accomplish this, our system of government will have to be corrupted. Make no mistake, there are people and organizations that would like to destroy our Constitution, our country, and our way of life. Be aware of subtle discussions being orchestrated by the media that help promote this incremental destruction. For instance, in a *Time* magazine article entitled "One Document, Under Siege"[111] (referring to the Constitution), the author questions the applicability of the Constitution in today's society and further suggests an implied elasticity. The article even goes as far as attacking our founders' wisdom by stating, "The framers were not gods and were not infallible," which is a not-so-subtle hint that the Constitution is not perfect.

> The powers not delegated to the United States by the Constitution, nor prohibited by it to the States, are reserved to the States respectively, or to the people.
>
> —US Constitution, Tenth Amendment

The article goes on to suggest that the Constitution was not meant to limit the powers of the federal government and even goes so far as to state the framers meant the exact opposite. While the article implies the Constitution is not in any danger, these subtle attacks open the door to discussion, which in time will get bolder, more aggressive, and more destructive.

In a heated interview about gay marriage between CNN Anchor Chris Cuomo and Alabama Chief Justice Roy Moore, Chris Cuomo stated, "Our rights do not come from God, your honor, and you know that. They come from man…That's your faith, that's my faith, but that's not our country. Our laws come from collective agreement and compromise."[112] This type of attack is yet another trial balloon by the agents of evil attempting to nip away at our Constitution and God-given rights. This should concern every freedom-loving American, religious or not.

On another front, expect Satan, with the aid of the media, to continue to cast a negative light on religion, with an emphasis on Christianity, and to use religious extremism in an attempt to make all religion look bad. For example, you may be familiar with the news story of the Jordanian pilot who was recently executed by Muslim extremists burning him alive while trapped in a cage. The president of the United States actually had the gall to imply a moral equivalency between these actions by Islamic terrorists and the Crusades. He actually drew a comparison between the atrocities of twenty-first-century Islamic extremists and the eleventh-century Crusades. Eventually, anyone reporting to have faith in God will be labeled an extremist and will be considered dangerous, with the ultimate goal of completely eliminating any public expression of faith so that any religious views, and thereby Christian views, cannot be expressed without ridicule, harassment, and possibly financial penalty.

Finally, don't be surprised when our leaders continue to implement new laws and programs that only exacerbate the problems they were trying to correct in the first place (e.g., welfare, Affordable Care Act, and so on). Be vigilant for any new programs that nip away at our individual liberties as well as nip away at our country's sovereignty and strength and weaken our national defense. If we continue down this path, eventually the love that is God will actually be treated as hate speech, and Christians may be prohibited from practicing and sharing their beliefs publicly in an attempt to eliminate Christianity through attrition.

> "So when you see the 'abomination of desolation,' spoken of by Daniel the prophet, standing where it ought not" (let the reader understand), "then let those who are in Judea flee to the mountains." (Mark 13:14)

Now Is the Time...

The simple believes every word, But the prudent considers well his steps. (Prov. 14:15)

Beloved, do not believe every spirit, but test the spirits, whether they are of God; because many false prophets have gone out into the world. (1 John 4:1)

As I researched many of the anti-Christian resources during the writing of this book, I found that many of them stated specifically that they analyzed the information from a Christian resource for you. In fact, many of them specifically state they have watched the film or read the book so that you do not have to waste your time. In other words, they do not want you to see for yourself. These are the same people who claim science is on their side.

When presented by themselves, it is easy to see why some anti-Christian resources are so convincing. They are able to make a compelling argument and present their case without allowing the opposition to rebut. But don't let others influence what you think and believe without question. Don't believe that a person has your best interest in mind just because of the group with which that person associates. Judge them by their actions and not just their words. This applies to science, religion, and especially politics. It is acceptable to trust, but you also need to verify. A person who lies about one thing will lie about others, and to Satan the ends justify the means. If you have doubts, listen to both sides of an argument, including what you consider the opposition, and see what they believe and try to understand why. If two sides say opposite things, then at least one of them is lying. Listening to both sides may make it easier to figure out which one. As a matter of fact, the anti-Christian resources are some of the best evidence for Christianity when you take the time to listen to both sides of the argument. Do a little research on your own, and you may discover some serious revelations about some people you believe to be your friends and representatives. With the omnipresence of the Internet, it is much easier to conduct research to help keep tabs on the truth. Conduct your own research and let the truth prevail.

> But you, O man of God, flee these things and pursue righteousness, godliness, faith, love, patience, gentleness. Fight the good fight of faith, lay hold on eternal life, to which you were also called and have confessed the good confession in the presence of many witnesses. (1 Tim. 6:11–12)

Dr. Ben Carson once told a joke about a talking bird. To paraphrase the story, a man bought a very expensive bird as a gift for his mother. This bird was amazing because of its talking abilities. The man sent the bird to his mother as a gift, and when he called to ask how she liked it, she stated, "It was delicious." The man went on to tell his mother about the bird's amazing abilities and how expensive it was. The mother responded by saying, "Well, he should have said something." Christians, being conservative in nature, have chosen to sit back and let our cultural heritage be stripped little by little. If we continue to be silent, don't be surprised as our culture becomes more evil (godless). Now is the time for Christians to stand up and be heard. Let us not be apathetic to the works of evil and take a step back to regain our cultural heritage. With a little effort, we can revert back to great courage and liberty rather than being on the verge of slavery and oppression.

> Now I urge you, brethren, note those who cause divisions and offenses, contrary to the doctrine which you learned, and avoid them. For those who are such do not serve our Lord Jesus Christ, but their own belly, and by smooth words and flattering speech deceive the hearts of the simple. (Rom. 16: 17–18)

We need to hold our representatives accountable and stop putting our faith in a political party rather than God. Don't expect politicians to necessarily have your best interests in mind. Ask yourself whether they represent you or whether their words and (more important) their actions are simply directed at holding on to their power. The same argument goes for the press. The United States would have the most effective and efficient government on the planet if the press did their jobs well and were not so biased. Our founders knew this when they penned the First Amendment to the Constitution, and that is why there is such a concerted effort to alter the Constitution today.

> One of the penalties for refusing to participate in politics is that you end up being governed by your inferiors.
>
> —(Attributed to) Plato

> When bad men combine, the good must associate; else they will fall one by one, an unpitied sacrifice in a contemptible struggle.
>
> —British statesman Edmund Burke

> (I)f the citizens neglect their duty and place unprincipled men in office, the government will soon be corrupted....If a republican government fails to secure public prosperity and happiness, it must be because the citizens neglect the Divine commands, and elect bad men to make and administer the laws.
>
> —Noah Webster

Not only do we need to hold our representatives and the press accountable, some of you may need to answer the call to serve. If men and women of good character shy away from these careers because of the negative associations, then don't be surprised if the men and women who fill them lack good character. There are some that suggest that the press, big banks, big industry, and politics are all controlled by the same few people with the same worldly agenda. If that is true, then they may also be controlling who runs and who wins political elections. We need good people to get involved who are willing to put God first in order to overcome these overwhelming odds.

†††

> Then He said to His disciples, "The harvest truly is plentiful, but the laborers are few. Therefore pray the Lord of the harvest to send out laborers into His harvest." (Matt. 9:37–38)

> And He said to them, "Go into all the world and preach the gospel to every creature." (Mark 16:15)

Do you ever sit around the dinner table and complain about politics but never do anything about it? Have you ever written your representatives? Have you ever written a letter to the editor? Have you ever signed a petition? Do you even bother to vote in the elections of your representatives? Approximately 60 percent of eligible voters participated in the last presidential election. That means 40 percent of eligible voters were either too apathetic or too lazy, and voter participation is even less in off-year elections. Don't you believe our country and our way of life are worth a little effort? Don't be put in the position of having to say, "If I had only…" because it may then be too late. Christians need to stop waiting in the wings as our rights are slowly stripped away. Christians are the majority, and we need to have a voice and not be intimidated by the negative tactics that have been used to keep us silent. We need men and women of good character to be our leaders and stand up for what is right rather than what is popular. We need to do the right thing for the right reason.

Even if you are a committed atheist, agnostic, or member of another faith, can you please explain why you are afraid of people with morals rooted in a belief in God? Why are you afraid of people committed to a belief in love, joy, peace, patience, kindness, goodness, faithfulness, gentleness, and self-control? I was once a committed atheist and evolutionist, and there was not even a single time I was ever offended, angry, or felt the least bit threatened by Christians. Even though I thought their beliefs to be silly at the time, they were almost always personable, likable, and overwhelmingly trustworthy people. While I did not share their beliefs, it was comforting to have people of character hanging around. Having Christians exercising their faith, especially through prayer, is not a threat to society or science.

Thus also faith by itself, if it does not have works, is dead. (James 2:17)

While the evidence cited in this text tends to point to some dire conditions, it is not too late. There have been some recent victories in the news that are good examples of how Christians can prevail if we just speak up and take action. Recall the attempted media lynching of Dan Cathy of Chick-fil-A. Nationwide boycotts were attempted in an effort to demonize him and his Christian beliefs, but the attempt backfired miserably with an overwhelming show of public support to the point the company was almost unable to keep up with the demand. People lined up to buy Chick-fil-A in record-setting numbers, with people standing in line for hours to show their support. Satan failed because good people stood up for what was right.

In an interview with *GQ* magazine, Duck Dynasty's Phil Robertson was asked what he thought about sin. He paraphrased a passage of the Bible that included, of course, that homosexuality is a sin. That interview led to the A&E network (temporarily) removing Mr. Robertson from the show. Due to another overwhelming show of public support, as well as support from his Christian family, the A&E network eventually recanted and allowed him to return to the show, although in this case it is not clear whether A&E's motives were based on the love of money or a reevaluation of their convictions. Either way, Satan failed because Christians stood up for what was right.

In these cases, Satan tried to go too far by overstepping the line, which resulted in a backlash by the American people who stood up to defend freedom. Beware, however; even when Satan fails, he is inching his way forward with each and every attempt. Satan's attacks were easily defeated today, but they might not be so easily defeated tomorrow. Things that are beyond the pale today may become mainstream in tomorrow's culture. For instance, can you imagine people fifty years ago allowing public schools to hand out free condoms to twelve-year-olds? Yet it is common today. Can you imagine people fifty years ago using public funds to pay for abortions on teenage girls without having to get the consent of their parents? Yet it is common today. Each time these attacks on our values occur, our culture inches away from God's Will for our lives.

Even if you don't believe in God and hold the neutral position of being agnostic, there is no harm in having the discussion or examining the evidence. Likewise, if you adhere to the religion of atheism, you can have the same tolerance for the Christian faith as you expect others to have for yours. There is absolutely no harm that can come from Christians praying or expressing their religious beliefs publicly. To try to pretend the First Amendment was meant to prevent religious expression is blatantly and obviously contrary to our founders' intentions to the point of being completely and absolutely absurd. Whether you are a believer, an agnostic, or an atheist, do you really want to go down a path where you are told what to think and what to do and say? Beware of this double-edged sword.

> If My people who are called by My name will humble themselves, and pray and seek My face, and turn from their wicked ways, then I will hear from heaven, and will forgive their sin and heal their land. (2 Chron. 7:14)

America has experienced three (some claim four) periods of great spiritual revival that have produced some remarkable and miraculous results. Those periods are referred to as the Great Awakenings. While each of the Great Awakenings covers a substantial length of time and history, the following text attempts to summarize them into just a few paragraphs to help illustrate the good that comes from putting God first.

The first Great Awakening occurred in the mid-eighteenth century, prior to the American Revolution, and is credited with initiating and promoting the democratic thought for our current system of government, the rule of law versus the rule of men. That thinking led to freedom of the press and freedom of religion, which are the cornerstones of our great country, and it eventually led to the American Revolution, which spawned the greatest country the world has ever seen. The concept of all men being created equal was first introduced into our culture during the first Great Awakening. This resulted in the conversion of slaves to Christianity, which eventually led to the education of slaves, a precursor to the abolition movement. An important emphasis in the first Great Awakening was the decentralization of religious information, the very foundation for religious freedom. The movement focused on a deep personal religious experience and the outpouring of the Holy Spirit, which was encouraged at the countless revivals occurring during that time.

The second Great Awakening occurred from the late eighteenth century to the mid-nineteenth century. Unlike the first Great Awakening that focused on the educated, the second Great Awakening included less-wealthy and less-educated people. The converts were primarily women and young people. In fact, the second Great Awakening inspired blacks to demand freedom and is attributed to leading to the abolition movement and equal rights for women. It also led to the reformation of prisons, care for the handicapped and mentally ill, and the formation of the religious and educational infrastructure that created and supported the most powerful and most prosperous nation in the world. More importantly, the second Great Awakening emphasized a deep personal relationship with Jesus Christ and resulted in millions of new converts.

The third Great Awakening occurred from the mid-nineteenth century through the early twentieth century. It helped prepare the nation for the bloodbath that was the Civil War and paved the way for the abolition of slavery. It was instrumental in getting us through one of the darkest times in American history, and we not only survived, but it also led to the coupling of the gospel to social work, which in turn created countless worldwide missionaries.

These spiritual awakenings were responsible for formation of the strongest, most productive, and most generous nation on the planet. Think about how awesome it would have been to be a part of these Great Awakenings, to have experienced God's power firsthand, and to have helped make this country what it is today. How awesome would it be to be a part of the next Great Awakening? Think about what it would take to start the next (and possibly final) Great Awakening. Wouldn't you like to be a part of that spiritual revival? Wouldn't it be great to see our country revert back to the principles it was founded upon? What would be the catalyst necessary to make it happen? If you think about it, there is really only one thing required...and that one thing is that *we* need to be doing God's Will for our lives.

> We must all hang together, or assuredly we shall all hang separately.
>
> —Benjamin Franklin, July 4, 1776

A few years back, a group of congressional representatives facing election got together and came up with a list of promises that they were committed to keep if elected. This election campaign actually worked, and they were able to keep the vast majority of those promises. If that were to happen today, what would you like to see on that list? What would be your top priorities? How about a commitment to the rule of law? How about a commitment to personal character in our representatives? How about a commitment to supporting our freedoms guaranteed by the Constitution? How about a commitment to personal and financial responsibility? How about a commitment to preserve our country and the system of government that so many people have died for? If you think about it, we could obtain all these things by simply restoring our Constitution, specifically, the rights memorialized in the First Amendment.

If we reverted back to the principles our country was founded upon, we could restore the United States to the beacon of liberty that we once were and maintain our leadership in the world for decades to come. If we reverted back to a trust in God rather than trust in government (people), all of those other things would simply fall into place. This is already the law; we just need to stop letting the tireless and vocal agents of Satan have their way.

> Because "All flesh is as grass, and all the glory of man as the flower of the grass. The grass withers, And its flower falls away, But the word of the Lord endures forever." Now this is the word which by the gospel was preached to you. (1 Pet. 1:24–25)

Who is the one person who had the most influence on our world and our culture? Obviously most Christians will say Jesus, but aside from Him, who would be your next pick? Stephen Hawking and Warren Buffett are two well-known people who have had worldwide influence for accomplishments in their respective fields. Stephen Hawking has been called the smartest man alive, and Warren Buffet is one of the richest. What if either or both of these men were to be touched by the Holy Spirit? Can you imagine the massive revival that would occur? Can you imagine the countless people either of these men could help lead to Christ if they gave their life to Jesus? What an incredible legacy that would be. In fifty years, science will have replaced Mr. Hawking several times over, and he will likely be all but forgotten. Likewise, as our culture progresses toward a more worldly focus, billionaires will come and go. Both of these men have an incredible once-in-a-millennium opportunity to change this world for the better and create a legacy that would forever mark our history. All they would have to do is seek God's Will for their lives.

Most notable world events begin by the most innocent of circumstances. What if something you did or said initiated the next Great Awakening? An innocent and simple gesture might possibly initiate an awareness of God like the world has never seen. What if you help lead someone to Christ that became the next Billy Graham? Again, what an incredible legacy it would be. We need to be living our lives for Christ and stand up to defend our faith because you never know what insignificant event may change our world for eternity. What is the One Thing you could do to change our world for the better?

> You cannot drink the cup of the Lord and the cup of demons; you cannot partake of the Lord's table and of the table of demons. (1 Cor. 10:21)

Our culture is moving more and more toward a worldly focus as we are taught to believe in worldly terms, which only serves to take us further away from the moral foundation that has been in place for centuries. We are further conditioned to believe that religion and the occult (evil) are myths or figments of our imaginations; therefore, there is nothing really to be applied in our everyday lives. But if you believe in God, then you must believe in Satan, and evil is not something we can afford to ignore. We need to be able to recognize Satan and evil in its many forms and either defeat it with the help of Jesus Christ or run away at the first sign of temptation. Better yet, avoid being put into situations that would tempt us in the first place. The world (Satan) is trying to hoodwink us into moving away from God, or at the very least require that we leave God at home or in our places of worship, which inhibits our ability to reach others for Christ.

Take a moment to compare the progress in our culture to the nine satanic statements from the Church of Satan and notice the progression toward indulgence instead of abstinence, selfishness rather than charity, science instead of faith, tolerance and encouraging of sin rather than personal responsibility, vengeance instead of forgiveness, dehumanization of the individual rather than sanctity of life, indulgence and embracing of sin (greed, lust, envy, anger, pride, sloth, and gluttony) rather than self-control, and finally, glorification of Satan and evil. Indeed, if Satan is real, how would he do it any differently?

> Little children, it is the last hour; and as you have heard that the Antichrist is coming, even now many antichrists have come, by which we know that it is the last hour. (1 John 2:18)

Friends, the hour is late. Our country and our world are on the precipice of being destroyed from within by every sort of evil, but it is not too late to make a difference. The fat lady has not yet sung, but she is dressed and clearing her throat.

As a final word of advice, as we move forward and progress in our culture, apply the theory and hypothesis postulated in the text of this book and see if the results don't support the same conclusion. If you deny God's existence, then you are blinding yourself to the existence of Satan and his influence. As long as you deny or ignore Satan's existence, he can influence your life in complete stealth and with total immunity. On the contrary, if you are aware of the nature of this negative life force, how much easier would it be to cope with? This war with evil is not bound by earthly means, and Satan does not play fair. We need God's help. If there is any portion of your life that you omit God, it provides Satan an opportunity.

The following paragraph is directed at Christians *only*, so any unbelievers can go ahead and skip to the next chapter.

So, for you believers out there, here is a thought for you to consider. If you really believe in Jesus Christ, what are you going to do about it? What do you believe is God's Will for your life? Go ahead and jot down your answer(s) and then consider this: There are a number of stories out there where people have died, gone to heaven, and then returned. Some examples are found in the book/movie *90 Minutes in Heaven* and the movie *Heaven Is for Real.* If you died and went to heaven and then by some miracle returned to this world, how would it affect your life? What would you be doing differently than you are doing right now? If there is a difference, why is that so? If there is a difference, then do you really believe? Think about it. The next Great Awakening may be waiting on you.

> And let us not grow weary while doing good, for in due season we shall reap if we do not lose heart. (Gal. 6:9)

HOPE

> Therefore submit to God. Resist the devil and he will flee from you. (James 4:7)

There are numerous stories in the Bible that chronicle Satan's influence, including stories where God has allowed His people to be manipulated, such as in the book of Job. However, because we are conditioned to believe that Satan and demons are myths, it is a little difficult to relate to these stories in today's culture. As a matter of fact, we would likely be considered crazy if we started blaming the devil or some supernatural force for our circumstances. But think about it for a moment and see if it doesn't explain a few things. How else can you explain the actions of James Eagan Holmes in the mass murder at the theater in Aurora, Colorado? How else can you explain the mass murder of twenty children and six adults at Sandy Hook Elementary School in Newtown, Connecticut? How else can you explain away the actions of Jim Jones and David Koresh and the resultant deaths of the followers of their respective cults? How else can you explain the pain, death, and destruction that are being perpetrated by ISIS/ISIL and their extremely cruel methodology? So if Satan is a relentless adversary, what can we do to protect ourselves against the forces of evil? Actually, the Bible very clearly provides the recipe.

> Finally, my brethren, be strong in the Lord and in the power of His might. Put on the whole armor of God, that you may be able to stand against the wiles of the devil. For we do not wrestle against flesh and

> blood, but against principalities, against powers, against the rulers of the darkness of this age, against spiritual hosts of wickedness in the heavenly places. Therefore take up the whole armor of God, that you may be able to withstand in the evil day, and having done all, to stand. Stand therefore, having girded your waist with truth, having put on the breastplate of righteousness, and having shod your feet with the preparation of the gospel of peace; above all, taking the shield of faith with which you will be able to quench all the fiery darts of the wicked one. And take the helmet of salvation, and the sword of the Spirit, which is the word of God; praying always with all prayer and supplication in the Spirit, being watchful to this end with all perseverance and supplication for all the saints. (Eph. 6:10–18)

So what is this armor of God referred to in the Scripture? Very simply, it's God's Word. Where can we find a reliable source of God's Word? Obviously, we should be reading the Bible and talking to God (praying)—daily. It is actually that simple. If there is an all-knowing God, the Creator of the universe, is it such a stretch that He would have provided a blueprint for how He wanted us to live our lives? If you think you know what God wants based on your personal definition of what is good without reading the Bible, you may be deluding yourself and be creating your own gospel. As a matter of fact, this would be a good test for your pastor and church. If the message that is being preached lacks appropriate biblical references and specifically omits Jesus, this may be an important clue that it is not from God. Beware, however; even the devil can cite Scripture to advance his agenda by manipulating the message, exactly like Jim Jones and David Koresh.

> Trust in the Lord with all your heart, And lean not on your own understanding; In all your ways acknowledge Him, And He shall direct your paths. (Prov. 3:5–6)

The first time or two of reading through the Bible, I actually had more questions than when I started. The references to slavery and conflict made it difficult to reconcile that there is an all-knowing, loving God of the universe.

Essentially, I wanted to understand Scripture before believing. However, this was a fundamental error on my part because understanding comes from believing, not the other way around. After discovering some of the different translations of the Bible, I began to understand some additional fundamental concepts. The Bible was interpreted from text that is thousands of years old, from cultures that were fundamentally different than our own. There are also many different translations of the Bible, which also adds to the confusion, and they all have their good points. With that said, it is worth offering an endorsement for the New English Translation (NET) because of its easy-to-read-and-understand format. Basically, the NET Bible is an endeavor to put biblical text into the language of our modern-day culture. It is a liberal rendering of the text that is translated thought by thought rather than word for word. While I actually prefer a more literal translation, the NET Bible goes beyond the call with thousands of translation notes, which help put the words into context. This is by no means to suggest it is the best translation, rather just to point out that the NET Bible is available in an easy-to-understand format and is available in electronic as well as printed form. As a matter of fact, there are many Internet resources that host multiple translations that can be viewed side by side, many of which are free to the user.

I would also recommend a study Bible, such as the Life Application Bible, which provides study notes on the vast majority of the text. These notes also help to provide context for the writings in easy-to-understand language. For instance, detractors would have us believe that Christianity is sexist because of some of the apostle Paul's writings about women (e.g., that they should be silent in church). Having appropriate study references helps keep those statements in the proper context, and the Life Application Bible comes in a variety of translations.

†††

> But sanctify the Lord God in your hearts, and always be ready to give a defense to everyone who asks you a reason for the hope that is in you, with meekness and fear; having a good conscience, that when

> they defame you as evildoers, those who revile your good conduct in Christ may be ashamed. (1 Pet. 3:15–16)

So what does the Bible say about the way we should live our lives? What does it mean to be a Christian? It's not an easy answer because the Bible is actually a collection of sixty-six books; nonetheless, let's examine select Scripture. These references are provided mostly for the nonbeliever but can be used by believers if and when Satan's accomplices attack you and your faith.

> Seek good and not evil, That you may live; So the Lord God of hosts will be with you, As you have spoken. (Amos 5:14)

> Depart from evil and do good; Seek peace and pursue it. (Ps. 34:14)

> "By this all will know that you are My disciples, if you have love for one another." (John 13:35)

> Let love be without hypocrisy. Abhor what is evil. Cling to what is good. Be kindly affectionate to one another with brotherly love, in honor giving preference to one another; not lagging in diligence, fervent in spirit, serving the Lord; rejoicing in hope, patient in tribulation, continuing steadfastly in prayer; distributing to the needs of the saints, given to hospitality. Bless those who persecute you; bless and do not curse. Rejoice with those who rejoice, and weep with those who weep. Be of the same mind toward one another. Do not set your mind on high things, but associate with the humble. Do not be wise in your own opinion. Repay no one evil for evil. Have regard for good things in the sight of all men. If it is possible, as much as depends on you, live peaceably with all men. Beloved, do not avenge yourselves, but rather give place to wrath; for it is written, "Vengeance is Mine, I will repay," says the Lord. Therefore "If your enemy is hungry, feed him; If he is thirsty, give him a drink; For in so doing you will heap

coals of fire on his head." Do not be overcome by evil, but overcome evil with good. (Rom. 12:9–21)

Let no one seek his own, but each one the other's well-being. (1 Cor. 10:24)

Love suffers long and is kind; love does not envy; love does not parade itself, is not puffed up; does not behave rudely, does not seek its own, is not provoked, thinks no evil; does not rejoice in iniquity, but rejoices in the truth; bears all things, believes all things, hopes all things, endures all things. (1 Cor. 13:4–7)

We are hard pressed on every side, yet not crushed; we are perplexed, but not in despair; persecuted, but not forsaken; struck down, but not destroyed—always carrying about in the body the dying of the Lord Jesus, that the life of Jesus also may be manifested in our body. (2 Cor. 4:8–10)

Do not be deceived, God is not mocked; for whatever a man sows, that he will also reap. For he who sows to his flesh will of the flesh reap corruption, but he who sows to the Spirit will of the Spirit reap everlasting life. And let us not grow weary while doing good, for in due season we shall reap if we do not lose heart. Therefore, as we have opportunity, let us do good to all, especially to those who are of the household of faith. (Gal. 6:7–10)

I, therefore, the prisoner of the Lord, beseech you to walk worthy of the calling with which you were called, with all lowliness and gentleness, with longsuffering, bearing with one another in love, endeavoring to keep the unity of the Spirit in the bond of peace. (Eph. 4:1–3)

Let him who stole steal no longer, but rather let him labor, working with his hands what is good, that he may have something to give him who has need. Let no corrupt word proceed out of your mouth, but what is good for necessary edification, that it may impart grace to the hearers. (Eph. 4:28–29)

Let all bitterness, wrath, anger, clamor, and evil speaking be put away from you, with all malice. And be kind to one another, tenderhearted, forgiving one another, just as God in Christ forgave you. (Eph. 4:31–32)

Let nothing be done through selfish ambition or conceit, but in lowliness of mind let each esteem others better than himself. Let each of you look out not only for his own interests, but also for the interests of others. Let this mind be in you which was also in Christ Jesus. (Phil. 2:3–5)

Rejoice in the Lord always. Again I will say, rejoice! Let your gentleness be known to all men. The Lord is at hand. Be anxious for nothing, but in everything by prayer and supplication, with thanksgiving, let your requests be made known to God; and the peace of God, which surpasses all understanding, will guard your hearts and minds through Christ Jesus. Finally, brethren, whatever things are true, whatever things are noble, whatever things are just, whatever things are pure, whatever things are lovely, whatever things are of good report, if there is any virtue and if there is anything praiseworthy—meditate on these things. The things which you learned and received and heard and saw in me, these do, and the God of peace will be with you. (Phil. 4:4–9)

But now you yourselves are to put off all these: anger, wrath, malice, blasphemy, filthy language out of your mouth. (Col. 3:8)

Therefore, as the elect of God, holy and beloved, put on tender mercies, kindness, humility, meekness, longsuffering; bearing with one another, and forgiving one another, if anyone has a complaint against another; even as Christ forgave you, so you also must do. But above all these things put on love, which is the bond of perfection. And let the peace of God rule in your hearts, to which also you were called in one body; and be thankful. Let the word of Christ dwell in you richly in all wisdom, teaching and admonishing one another in psalms and hymns and spiritual songs, singing with grace in your hearts to the Lord. And whatever you do in word or deed, do all in the name of the Lord Jesus, giving thanks to God the Father through Him. (Col. 3:12–17)

Walk in wisdom toward those who are outside, redeeming the time. Let your speech always be with grace, seasoned with salt, that you may know how you ought to answer each one. (Col. 4:5–6)

Finally, brethren, pray for us, that the word of the Lord may run swiftly and be glorified, just as it is with you, and that we may be delivered from unreasonable and wicked men; for not all have faith. But the Lord is faithful, who will establish you and guard you from the evil one. (2 Thess. 3:1–3)

And a servant of the Lord must not quarrel but be gentle to all, able to teach, patient, in humility correcting those who are in opposition, if God perhaps will grant them repentance, so that they may know the truth, and that they may come to their senses and escape the snare of the devil, having been taken captive by him to do his will. (2 Tim. 2:24–26)

Therefore, laying aside all malice, all deceit, hypocrisy, envy, and all evil speaking. (1 Pet. 2:1)

Finally, all of you be of one mind, having compassion for one another; love as brothers, be tenderhearted, be courteous; not returning evil

> for evil or reviling for reviling, but on the contrary blessing, knowing that you were called to this, that you may inherit a blessing. For "He who would love life And see good days, Let him refrain his tongue from evil, And his lips from speaking deceit. Let him turn away from evil and do good; Let him seek peace and pursue it. For the eyes of the Lord are on the righteous, And His ears are open to their prayers; But the face of the Lord is against those who do evil." (1 Pet. 3:8–12)

So again, based on what it really means to be a Christian (according to biblical text), can someone please explain why Christianity is under such an all-out attack? Why is there such a concerted effort to limit religious expression? Why would anyone find these personal values to be so offensive?

> What shall we say then? Is the law sin? Certainly not! On the contrary, I would not have known sin except through the law. For I would not have known covetousness unless the law had said, "You shall not covet." (Rom. 7:7)

The fact is, the very definition of what our culture considers good versus evil was originally based on biblical principles. If our morality does not come from God, then it comes from collective agreement and compromise and is subject to change at any time.

> Let no corrupt word proceed out of your mouth, but what is good for necessary edification, that it may impart grace to the hearers. (Eph. 4:29)

You have undoubtedly seen fictional stories where a character is contemplating a course of action and the character's good side and dark side of his or her conscience is displayed as an angel on one shoulder and a devil on the other. While this scenario has typically been used for humor's sake, in reality, it can be very descriptive of what actually may be happening in real life, at least from a practical sense. For instance, think about the ease with which people go out of their way to be offended and take words and actions the wrong way. This includes people from all walks of life, including people you work with, go to church with, friends, and even family. It is amazing how easily people are offended in today's society. How many times have you or someone you know taken offense to the statements of others because they heard or read their statements incorrectly? Sometimes those interpretations may be reasonable based on what was said; nonetheless, how often are they a complete distortion of what was meant to be conveyed?

I often use too few words to convey a thought, which sometimes leaves my words open to interpretation. On the other hand, I do not have a malicious bone in my body, and it boggles my mind when people who know me assume that I have said something offensive. Even on those occasions when others' words are specifically meant to offend, the Bible clearly states that we are not to return evil for evil, and we are commanded to bless our enemies. Which side of your conscience do you think is creating these negative thoughts? Which side of your conscience are you listening to?

There have been countless times when things do not go the way I want or expect, and it has, on occasion, offended my ego. Nonetheless, I have learned to ignore these attempts by Satan to influence my understanding, words, and actions. I have learned to be encouraging rather than discouraging, to be thankful rather than resentful, and to be optimistic rather than pessimistic (even when I don't feel like it). This understanding has improved my life beyond words.

So how does knowing there is a dark side trying to influence your thoughts and actions help you cope with evil? Let's use another Hollywood example to help illustrate. There is an episode in the original *Star Trek* series called "The Day of the Dove,"[113] where an evil entity infiltrates the starship *Enterprise* and feeds on hate and conflict. In this episode, the entity has the capability of creating illusions in its victims' minds that manifest and encourage hate and prejudice, thereby producing negative reactions that perpetuate the cycle. Sound familiar? The entity continuously pits the Federation crew against a crew of Klingons in hand-to-hand combat as it feeds on the ensuing hate and carnage that are produced. It is not until after the characters discover the existence of the entity and its motives that they are effective in defending themselves. Both adversaries refuse to be manipulated by the evil entity and lay down their arms. Think about this from a biblical perspective. Are you letting Satan manipulate your actions, your relationships, and your life with lies and deceit? Imagine the fun Satan is having every time he gets the best of you.

As a Christian believer, how do you respond to Satan and his influence? Have you been desensitized to his works to the point that you are no longer on guard against his influence? How many times have you rationalized this one sin or that one sin won't hurt anybody because God is a forgiving God? Have you ever lied, cheated, stolen, partaken in sexual immorality, or committed any other sin? Do you use pornography, believing it is OK this one time? Can you rationalize an extramarital affair as being OK because you believe God wants you to be happy? Do you eat or drink too much or take drugs? If you are a believer, why are you not terrified by Satan's attempts at influencing your life? Every time we give in to sin, we are giving in to Satan, which only strengthens him and takes us farther from God's Will for our lives. It is true that through Jesus Christ all sin is forgiven, but as a Christian you cannot use this as a trump card to live life as you want.

We need to stop listening to the dark side of our consciences. The more Satan attacks you, be comforted in knowing that you are on the right path. In a way, it has helped me in my walk with the Lord by making it easier to avoid temptation. I have experienced many temptations during the writing of this book and could see Satan's fingerprints all over those circumstances, which made it much easier to resist. The more Satan tries to influence me, the stronger my faith becomes and the more certain I am on the right path. As a matter of fact, this may be a good deterrent for Satan. If he knows that his attacks only strengthen your faith, he may decide it is better to leave you alone. While we likely cannot keep Satan from ever having an effect on our lives, we can control how we respond to that influence.

> Be anxious for nothing, but in everything by prayer and supplication, with thanksgiving, let your requests be made known to God. (Phil. 4:6)

Remember, in any portion of your life that you omit God, it provides Satan an opportunity. Pray about everything and seek God's providence in everything you do and say, both at home and in public. Our Founding Fathers never intended for our country to be void of religious expression. We need to stand up for our rights and defend our liberties; else we will lose them.

> And you will be hated by all for My name's sake. But he who endures to the end shall be saved. (Mark 13:13)

What Is Keeping You from God?

If you have lived anywhere in the civilized world, you are most likely familiar with Christian beliefs. If you have Christian relatives, friends, and acquaintances, there is a likelihood they have attempted to be a witness for Jesus Christ at one time or another. If so, how did you respond to this witness? Are you respectful of others' beliefs, or did you avoid the conversation? Are you receptive to the Christian message, or has Satan hardened your heart?

What would Satan have to do to keep you away from discovering the True Jesus, the only path to God? Depending on many factors, obviously, the level of effort required varies tremendously from person to person. Someone who is convinced that there is no such thing as an all-knowing God requires significantly less of Satan's effort and may be much easier to manipulate than someone who was raised in a Christian family.

> O Timothy! Guard what was committed to your trust, avoiding the profane and idle babblings and contradictions of what is falsely called knowledge—by professing it some have strayed concerning the faith. Grace be with you. Amen. (1 Tim. 6:20–21)

I have a scientist friend and colleague that holds science in such reverence, he has essentially elevated it to his own pseudoreligion. He even tithes to science by buying carbon offsets to try to help save the planet (which I assume gives him some sort of peace of mind). For some reason God has put it on my heart to pray for this man, and I have attempted to witness to him on several occasions. However, most of those discussions never develop into adult conversations because he is so convinced that there is no God and he is so prejudiced against anything related to Christianity that he does not want to spend even a brief moment to discuss it. Any attempt at discussing religion, especially Christianity, is met by a solid wall of resistance, which immediately ends the conversation.

Now this is why I have such a problem with this man's beliefs. Regardless of his personal convictions, religion has a significant role in our culture, and the vast majority of people around the world believe in a deity of some sort. If he is truly a scientist, then he should at least be open to examining the evidence. But he is so hard-hearted, he will not open his mind enough to even consider the existence of God. He not only rejects any evidence that might support an argument for one, but he refuses to even hear it. This type of person is Satan's easiest victim. Satan does not need to spend much time or effort trying to keep this man from discovering the Truth; however, it certainly appears that Satan does spend a lot of time tormenting this troubled soul. From my countless water-cooler discussions with him over the years, it appears his life is almost void of any joy and almost every single day is the worst day of his life. I can't count the number of times he has stated, "I have never seen it this bad before." But please do not get me wrong. I truly believe he is incredibly intelligent, and I do like him personally. If there were anyone that could ever use a relationship with Jesus, this man could; however, it may never happen because he won't even allow the conversation to take place. Wouldn't you think a really smart person could engage in the conversation and at least investigate why so many others hold these beliefs?

As futile as it seems to me, God has put it on my heart to pray for this associate, and there has to be a reason for that. And while it does appear to be pointless, I am comforted in knowing that all things are possible with God. After all, I used to hold similar beliefs, and if there is hope for me, then there is hope for anybody. By the way, you will see a grown man cry the day that I discover this friend and colleague has accepted Christ as his Savior.

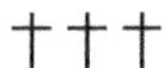

> For all have sinned and fall short of the glory of God. (Rom. 3:23)

Do people who refer to themselves as Christians make you want to run from religion? Do they do things that turn you off? Do they do things that you believe aren't Christlike? Do you blame their religious beliefs and therefore don't want to be like them? If so, don't be fooled. All people are sinners, including all Christians, and we are all tempted by worldly things. Don't be turned off to Christianity just because someone who claims to be a Christian does not act the way you expect a Christian to act. That is exactly what Satan wants you to think; although, it is true that the church is filled with hypocrites. We do not always practice what we preach, but it is our desire to become more Christlike. Besides, not going to church because there are sinners is like not going to the hospital because there are sick people.

> And again He began to teach by the sea. And a great multitude was gathered to Him, so that He got into a boat and sat in it on the sea; and the whole multitude was on the land facing the sea. Then He taught them many things by parables, and said to them in His teaching: "Listen! Behold, a sower went out to sow. And it happened, as he sowed, that some seed fell by the wayside; and the birds of the air came and devoured it. Some fell on stony ground, where it did not have much earth; and immediately it sprang up because it had no depth of earth. But when the sun was up it was scorched, and because it had no root it withered away. And some seed fell among thorns; and the thorns grew up and choked it, and it yielded no crop. But other seed fell on good ground and yielded a crop that sprang up, increased and produced: some thirtyfold, some sixty, and some a hundred." And He said to them, "He who has ears to hear, let him hear!" (Mark 4:1–9)

I can speak from experience about the many things that had kept me away from God and out of church for many years. The first and most toxic was a direct result of too much testosterone. In my youth, I wanted to do my own thing and did not want to be held to any outdated, square standard, especially when it came to girls. The tragedy surrounding Jim Jones and the Jonestown massacre also caused me to run away from religion as fast as I could. At the time, I thought it was better not to even try than to take a chance on connecting with a cult like the Peoples Temple. My previous beliefs that science and the Bible were mutually exclusive also kept me from investigating God for a very long time. As a geology major in college, I encountered a biology professor that ridiculed anyone that even hinted about a belief in God. I found his arguments for evolution to be compelling because they were being taught as fact, and I did not bother to question them. At that time, I believed people of faith were weak and needed something else in their lives, and to give in meant that I was weak. Pride and ignorance kept me away so I could continue to live the way I wanted, and I did not bother to listen to the other side. Sound familiar?

It was much later on in my adult life that I met my good friend and coworker Glen, who first planted the seeds of salvation into my heart that actually took root. Then I met my future wife, who saw me for the man I was meant to be and nurtured those seeds until they finally produced the fruits of the Spirit. These two people cared enough about me to share the gospel despite the overwhelming odds against their success. Do you care enough about others to expend a little effort toward the Great Commission? Words cannot describe how grateful I am that so many people cared enough about me to share the gospel. And believe me, I did not always show my appreciation. As a matter of fact, Glen and I parted company long before I became a Christian, so he never actually got to see the fruits of his labor.

For where your treasure is, there your heart will be also. (Luke 12:34)

So be honest. What does Satan have to do to keep you from discovering God? Does the love of money have you preoccupied? Are you too busy with your career? Do material things consume your thoughts? Do you spend all of your spare time watching TV? Is sex more important to you than your immortal soul? Are you letting the lies, deceit, and trickery of the master deceiver keep you from the Truth? Take a step back and examine yourself and then lose those barriers. Even if you are convinced there is no God, there is certainly no harm in researching Christianity so that you may understand the beliefs of the vast majority of Americans. Why avoid the conversation? Or are you afraid of what you will discover?

> You will know them by their fruits. Do men gather grapes from thorn bushes or figs from thistles? Even so, every good tree bears good fruit, but a bad tree bears bad fruit. A good tree cannot bear bad fruit, nor can a bad tree bear good fruit. Every tree that does not bear good fruit is cut down and thrown into the fire. Therefore by their fruits you will know them. (Matt. 7:16–20)

As a final plea, please consider the two following opposing questions:

1) What if you are wrong about your nonbelief and there really is a God of the Bible?
2) What if you gave your life to Christ and there really is no God?

Let's follow the flowchart and contemplate the possibilities.

1) If you are wrong about your nonbelief and there really is a God,
    - you will have wasted your life pursuing treasures on earth, where moth and rust destroy and where thieves break in and steal;
    - you will have missed the opportunity to experience the peace that comes with salvation and living a life for Christ. Even if you believe you have led a happy life, imagine what it could have been if you had known Christ as your Savior;
    - you will have missed the joy that comes from knowing and worshiping our Lord;

- you will have missed the fellowship with other believers and sense of family that it brings;
- you will have missed having purpose for your life and the opportunity for it to have more meaning than just living for the day;
- you will have missed the opportunity to share your faith and to help others to discover the Truth; and
- most important, you will ultimately spend an eternity separated from God. While theologians can debate what that really means, we can at least agree it is a really bad thing.

And that is just to name a few.

2) On the other hand, if you gave your life to Christ and there really is no God,
    - you will have lived your life with purpose based on a philosophy of putting others before yourself;
    - you will have spent your time and money helping others based on a philosophy that makes you feel really good about yourself and those around you;
    - you will have spent your time in meditation (prayer) contemplating all of the many blessings you have in your life and how to become a better person;
    - you will have experienced the joy of fellowship and worship and shared that joy with countless others;
    - you will have experienced the family that comes with the fellowship of believers;
    - you will have lived your life with a hope and faith that nobody could take from you;
    - you will have had a character that was based on something other than what was popular or politically correct; and
    - when you die, you will cease to exist, and you won't be spending eternity wondering what life could have been had you only known the Truth.

Given these possibilities, what is it that scares you away from God? What is it that you think you might be missing if you gave your life to Christ? What is the real downside here? Living a life for Christ would in no way limit your potential, and as a matter of fact, your true potential can only be found through Christ.

> The devil, who deceived them, was cast into the lake of fire and brimstone where the beast and the false prophet are. And they will be tormented day and night forever and ever. (Rev. 20:10)

If you are still not convinced that Satan is real and therefore there is a God in heaven, as our culture continues down this dark path, you will know this text to be true when:

- Christians lose their businesses because of the intolerant abuses of the politically correct;
- politicians are allowed to break the law and not be held accountable;
- patriotism becomes a vice;
- there are more encroachments limiting our liberty of free speech;
- our citizens continue to become more hopelessly dependent on government assistance;
- our culture incites more and more division, particularly between races;
- churches lose their tax-exempt status;
- Christian pastors are forced to perform homosexual weddings (and there are no corresponding actions against Islam or any other religion);
- seminaries are forced to admit homosexuals and transgendereds;
- our culture punishes initiative and rewards sloth;
- our medical profession devalues human life by assisting people to commit suicide;
- our culture abandons and removes our historical monuments because of their association to Christianity;

- the United States abandons Israel as an ally;
- pornography becomes mainstream;
- abortion clinics harvest aborted baby parts for sale;
- our courts rule the Constitution is unconstitutional;
- major incidents, such as natural disasters, terrorist activity, pandemics, or mass shootings, are used to justify more and more encroachment on our civil liberties; and
- the agents of Satan attack this book, its author, and his family.

When these things happen, you will know for certain that Satan is real, and the only hope is through our Lord Jesus Christ. Be prepared for Satan and his agenda, and have no fellowship with the unfruitful works of darkness, but rather expose them.

God bless you.

END NOTES

1. "Beyond a Reasonable Doubt," *The Free Dictionary by Farlex, Legal Dictionary*, http://legal-dictionary.thefreedictionary.com/Beyond+a+Reasonable+Doubt.

2. George Clooney as Ulysses Everett McGill, *O Brother, Where Art Thou?,* based on *The Odyssey,* by Homer, written and directed by Joel and Ethan Coen, DVD, 2000, listed at http://www.imdb.com/title/tt0190590/.

3. The Church of Jesus Christ of Latter-Day Saints, https://www.mormon.org/.

4. Dan Arel, "Why Bill Nye Shouldn't Debate Ken Ham," Richard Dawkins Foundation, January 16, 2014, https://richarddawkins.net/2014/01/why-bill-nye-shouldnt-debate-ken-ham/.

5. *Expelled: No Intelligence Allowed*, written by Kevin Miller and Ben Stein, directed by Nathan Frankowski, 2008, listed at http://www.imdb.com/title/tt1091617/.

6. "Definition of Intelligent Design," *Intelligent Design*, http://www.intelligentdesign.org/whatisid.php.

7. *Creatures That Defy Evolution,* 3-volume DVD set, narrated by Dr. Jobe Martin, http://www.explorationfilms.com/exploration-films-incredible-creatures-3.html.

8. Charles Darwin, M.A., *On the Origin of Species,* Kindle Edition (based on first edition), ASIN: B008478VE8, http://www.amazon.com/origin-species-Charles-Darwin-ebook/dp/B008478VE8/ref=sr_1_2?s=digital-text&ie=UTF8&qid=1451593777&sr=1-2&keywords=on+origin+of+species.

9. "Is God Dead?" *Time Magazine*, April 8, 1966, http://content.time.com/time/magazine/article/0,9171,835309,00.html.

10. "Does God Exist?," hosted by Martin Bashir, *Nightline,* Faceoff, ABC News, May 9, 2007, http://abcnews.go.com/Nightline/video/full-face-off-god-exist-3156022 https://www.youtube.com/watch?v=OPJ6ece-rII.

11. *The Blasphemy Challenge*, http://www.blasphemychallenge.com.

12. "Does Satan Exist?," hosted by Dan Harris, *Nightline,* Faceoff, ABC News, March 20, 2009, http://abcnews.go.com/Nightline/video/part-satan-exist-7185569.

13. Ken Ham and Bill Nye, *Creation vs. Evolution,* debate hosted by Tom Forman in Legacy Hall of the Creation Museum in Hebron, Kentucky, February 4, 2014, https://www.youtube.com/watch?v=z6kgvhG3AkI.

14. Michael Lipka, "7 facts about atheists," *Pew Research Center,* November 5, 2015 http://www.pewresearch.org/fact-tank/2015/11/05/7-facts-about-atheists/.

15. Saul Alinsky, *Rules for Radicals,* published by Vintage books/Random House, 1971, dedication page. ISBN-10: 0679721134, ISBN-13: 978-0679721130, http://www.amazon.com/Rules-Radicals-Practical-Primer-Realistic/dp/0679721134.

16. Anton Szandor LaVey, "The Nine Satanic Statements," Church of Satan, http://www.churchofsatan.com/nine-satanic-statements.php.

17. "Wicca," *Wikipedia*, https://en.wikipedia.org/wiki/Wicca.

18. "A Brief History of Wicca," *Church and School of Wicca,* http://www.wicca.org/Church/WiccaOutline.html.

19. Wiccan Rede, *Church and School of Wicca,* home page, http://wicca.org/.

20. *Religulous*, directed by Larry Charles, hosted by Bill Maher, 2008, listed at http://www.imdb.com/title/tt0815241/.

21. José Luis de Jesús, *Wikipedia*, https://en.wikipedia.org/wiki/Jos%C3%A9_Luis_de_Jes%C3%BAs

22. "Bill Maher—Views and Beliefs: Religion," *Wikipedia*, https://en.wikipedia.org/wiki/Bill_Maher.

23. Rod Serling, "The Howling Man," *The Twilight Zone,* season 2, episode 5, directed by Douglas Heyes, 1960, listed at http://www.imdb.com/title/tt0734645/.

24. James Madison, Speech at the Virginia Convention to Ratify the Federal Constitution (1788-06-06), *The Federalist Papers,* https://www.thefederalistpapers.org/founders/james-madison-quotes.

25. Obesity and Overweight, *Centers for Disease Control and Prevention,* Adults, http://www.cdc.gov/nchs/fastats/obesity-overweight.htm

26. Number of Abortions—Abortions Counter (as of December 2015), http://www.numberofabortions.com/.

27. Planned Parenthood Tweet on January 22, 2014, https://twitter.com/ppact/status/426000248008241152.

28. Chloe Angyal, "HAPPY 41ST BIRTHDAY, ROE V WADE," 2014, *Feministing,* http://feministing.com/2014/01/22/happy-41st-birthday-roe-v-wade/.

29. Ray Comfort, *180 Movie*, 2011, http://www.180movie.com/.

30. United Nations Global Commission on HIV and the Law, "Rights, Risks, and Health," July 2012, http://www.hivlawcommission.org/resources/report/FinalReport-Risks, Rights&Health-EN.pdf.

31. *For the Bible Tells Me So,* written by Daniel G. Karslake and Helen R. Mendoza, directed by Daniel G. Karslake, 2007, as listed at http://www.imdb.com/title/tt0912583/.

32. Presbyterianism and homosexuality, *Wikipedia,* https://en.wikipedia.org/wiki/Presbyterianism_and_homosexuality.

33. Michael Swift, *The Homosexual Manifesto,* reprinted from *The Congressional Record of the United States Congress*; first printed in *Gay Community News,* February 15–21, 1987; http://www.massresistance.org/docs/gen/09b/Redeeming_rainbow/chapters/Chapter-13.pdf.

34. National Vital Statistics Report, Volume 62, Number 9, "Births: Final Data for 2012," *Centers for Disease Contol,* December 30, 2013 http://www.cdc.gov/nchs/data/nvsr/nvsr62/nvsr62_09.pdf.

35. Patrick F. Fagan, "Rising Illegitimacy: America's Social Catastrophe," Heritage Foundation, F.Y.1. No. 19, June 29, 1994, http://www.heritage.org/research/reports/1994/06/rising-illegitimacy.

36. Jessica Bennett and Jesse Ellison, "The Case Against Marriage," *Newsweek,* June 11, 2010, http://www.newsweek.com/case-against-marriage-73045.

37. Robert Rector, "The New Federal Wedding Tax: How Obamacare Would Dramatically Penalize Marriage," Heritage Foundation WebMemo #2767 on Family and Marriage, January 20, 2010, http://www.heritage.org/research/reports/2010/01/the-new-federal-wedding-tax-how-obamacare-would-dramatically-penalize-marriage#.UlHmSLFLQ1A.facebook.

38. Dr. Rober Lefever, After a five-year-old becomes the youngest known child to be diagnosed with Gender Identity Disorder, just when is a boy a girl?," *THE DAILY MAIL,* update February 21, 2012 http://www.

dailymail.co.uk/debate/article-2104248/As-Zach-Avery-5-youngest-child-diagnosed-Gender-Identity-Disorder-just-boy-girl.html.

39. Dr. Lyndsey Myskow, "Five is old enough to know what gender you are," Mirror, February 21, 2012. http://www.mirror.co.uk/news/uk-news/five-is-old-enough-to-know-what-692478.

40. Josh Levs, "California Governor OKs Ban on Gay Conversion Therapy, Calling It 'Quackery,'" CNN.com, October 2, 2012, http://www.cnn.com/2012/10/01/us/california-gay-therapy-ban/index.html.

41. Roger Gitlin, "The State of California's Assault on Family Values Continues into 2012," canadafreepress.com, January 8, 2012, http://canadafreepress.com/article/the-state-of-californias-assault-on-family-values-continues-into-2012.

42. Bill Chappell, *NPR,* Germany Offers Third Gender Option On Birth Certificates, updated November 1, 2013, published November 1, 2013, http://www.npr.org/sections/thetwo-way/2013/11/01/242366812/germany-offers-third-gender-option-on-birth-certificates.

43. "Sex and gender diverse passport applicants," Australian Government, Department of Foreign Affairs and Trade, Passports Explained: The application process: Eligibility and identity overview, https://www.passports.gov.au/passportsexplained/theapplicationprocess/eligibilityoverview/Pages/changeofsexdoborpob.aspx.

44. Emily Alpert Reyes, "Transgender Study Looks at 'Exceptionally High' Suicide-Attempt Rate," *Los Angeles Times*, January 28, 2014, http://articles.latimes.com/2014/jan/28/local/la-me-ln-suicide-attempts-alarming-transgender-20140127.

45. Sarah Boesveld, "Becoming disabled by choice, not chance: 'Transabled' people feel like impostors in their fully working bodies," *National Post,*

June 3, 2015 http://news.nationalpost.com/news/canada/becoming-disabled-by-choice-not-chance-transabled-people-feel-like-impostors-in-their-fully-working-bodies.

46. Thaddeus Baklinski, "Delaware: 1st State to Jail Parents Who Use Spanking to Discipline," lifesitenews.com, September 26, 2012, https://www.lifesitenews.com/news/delaware-1st-state-to-jail-for-parents-who-use-spanking-to-discipline.

47. SENATE BILL NO. 234, Delaware State Senate, 146th General Assembly, http://www.legis.delaware.gov/LIS/lis146.nsf/vwLegislation/SB+234/$file/legis.html?open.

48. Arnold Ahlert, "Helicopter Parents? Helicopter Government Is More Like It," *Patriot Post,* April 20, 2015, http://patriotpost.us/articles/34712.

49. Arnold Ahlert, "Destroying the Family to Achieve Utopia," *Patriot Post,* May 11, 2015, http://patriotpost.us/articles/35121.

50. Jill Tucker, "Oakland to Halt School Suspensions for Willful Defiance," sfgate.com, May 14, 2015, http://www.sfgate.com/bayarea/article/Oakland-to-halt-school-suspensions-for-willful-6262461.php.

51. Jason Howerton, "'Non-Discrimination Policy' Results in Girls as Young as 6-Years-Old Being Allegedly Exposed to 'Male Genitalia' in Women's Locker Room," *The Blaze,* November 2, 2012, http://www.theblaze.com/stories/2012/11/02/non-discrimination-policy-results-in-girls-as-young-as-6-years-old-being-allegedly-exposed-to-male-genitalia-in-womens-locker-room/.

52. *Library of Congress*, Religion and the Founding of the American Republic, Religion and the Congress of the Confederation, "The Liberty Window," July 9, 1776, http://www.loc.gov/exhibits/religion/rel04.html.

53. *The Declaration of Independence,* July 4, 1776, http://www.archives.gov/exhibits/charters/declaration_transcript.html.

54. *Library of Congress*, Religion and the Founding of the American Republic, Religion and the Congress of the Confederation, "Congressional Fast Day Proclamation," May 17, 1776, http://www.loc.gov/exhibits/religion/rel04.html.

55. *Library of Congress,* Religion and the Founding of the American Republic, Religion and the Congress of the Confederation, "Congressional Thanksgiving Day Proclamation," December 18, 1777, http://www.loc.gov/exhibits/religion/rel04.html.

56. Wall Builders, *Aiken Bible*, http://www.wallbuilders.com/libissuesarticles.asp?id=46.

57. *Library of Congress*, "Thanksgiving, Founders Give Thanks," October 11, 1782, http://www.loc.gov/teachers/classroommaterials/presentationsandactivities/presentations/thanksgiving/.

58. United States Constitution, September 17, 1787, US Government Publishing Office, http://www.gpo.gov/fdsys/pkg/GPO-CONAN-1992/pdf/GPO-CONAN-1992-6.pdf.

59. "Public Worship at the U.S. Capitol," *Lost Episodes in American History,* March 21, 2013, http://lostepisodes.us/public-worship-at-the-capitol/.

60. David Barton, "Church in the U.S. Capitol," *Wall Builders,* November 10, 2005, http://www.wallbuilders.com/libissuesarticles.asp?id=46.

61. George J. Olszewski, "A History of the WASHINGTON MONUMENT 1844–1968 Washington, D.C.," April 1971, http://theroadtoemmaus.org/RdLb/21PbAr/Hst/US/WashMonCap.htm http://theroadtoemmaus.org/.

62. "George Washington," General Orders, May 2, 1778, *Founding Father Quotes,* http://www.foundingfatherquotes.com/father/quotes/5.

63. Samuel Adams, *The Writings of Samuel Adams,* volume IV. 1778–1802, p. 189, https://books.google.com/books?id=6pILAAAAIAAJ&printsec=frontcover&dq=the+writings+of+samuel+adams&hl=en&sa=X&ved=0ahUKEwjYyMvMzM3JAhXSpIMKHeHrD_cQ6AEINTAB#v=onepage&q=the%20writings%20of%20samuel%20adams&f=false.

64. Benjamin Franklin, *Benjamin Franklin, Autobiography and Other Writings on Politics, Economics, and Virtue,* edited by Alan Houston, Cambridge University Press, p. 4, https://books.google.com/books?id=VzmIi8juxwoC&printsec=frontcover&source=gbs_ge_summary_r&cad=0#v=onepage&q&f=false.

65. James Madison, "James Madison Quotes," Letter to Rev. Frederick Beasley (1825-11-20), *The Federalist Papers,* https://www.thefederalist-papers.org/founders/james-madison-quotes.

66. Alexander Hamilton, "Alexander Hamilton, The Farmer Refuted," The Founders' Constitution, Volume 1, Chapter 3, Document 5 Papers 1:86--89, 121--22, 135—36 February 23, 1775, http://press-pubs.uchicago.edu/founders/documents/v1ch3s5.html.

67. Thomas Paine, "Common Sense," *Thomas Paine, The Writings of Thomas Paine, Vol. I (1774–1779) [1774],* January 1776, http://oll.libertyfund.org/quote/308.

68. Calvin Coolidge, "Significant Papers" by Cal Thomas, *The Coolidge Foundation,* coolidgefoundation.org, https://coolidgefoundation.org/resources/significant-papers-7/.

69. Abraham Lincoln, *Record of Christian Work,* W. R. Moody, editor, A. P. Fitt, managing editor, p. 220, volume 41, 1922, https://books.google.com/books?id=FKhVAAAAYAAJ&pg=PA359&lpg=PA359&dq=Record+of+Christian+Work,+W.+R.+Moody&source=bl&ots=C7zJ7xJn0a&sig=558vI-ydI-IISP4zXIjDp_ovuSw&hl=en&sa=X&ved=0ahUKEwiO_YbRhofKAhVMGT4KHbkTDpcQ6AEIKTAC#v=onepage&q&f=false.

70. Franklin D. Roosevelt, letter to the troops, *The Federalist Papers Project,* "The Franklin Delano Roosevelt Military Pocket Bible," article by Steve Straub, http://www.thefederalistpapers.org/us/the-franklin-delano-roosevelt-military-pocket-bible.

71. Virginia Declaration of Rights, Article 16, June 12, 1776, http://www.archives.gov/exhibits/charters/virginia_declaration_of_rights.html.

72. Massachusetts Constitution of 1780, PT. 1 Handlin 442–48, "Part the First. A Declaration of the Rights of the Inhabitants of the Commonwealth of Massachusetts," Article II, 1780, http://press-pubs.uchicago.edu/founders/documents/bill_of_rightss6.html.

73. *Library of Congress,* "Jefferson's Letter to the Danbury Baptists," January 1, 1802, https://www.loc.gov/loc/lcib/9806/danpre.html.

74. *The First Atheist Church of True Science,* http://www.factschurch.com/.

75. 370 US 421, 82 S. Ct. 1261, 8 L. Ed. 2d 601—Supreme Court, 1962.

76. *PROFILES OF PERPETRATORS OF TERRORISM—UNITED STATES (PPT-US),* Chapter 12: Subideology, January 30, 2012, p. 18, http://info.publicintelligence.net/START-US-TerrorismProfiles.pdf.

77. "Anti-Christian Persecution & Oppression in Canada," *Campaign Life Coalition,* http://www.campaignlifecoalition.com/shared/media/editor/file/PersecutionOfChristians(1).pdf.

78. (Attributed to) Alexander Fraser Tytler, *Wikipedia,* Cycle of Freedom, https://en.wikipedia.org/wiki/Alexander_Fraser_Tytler.

79. Mike Huckabee commentary, Fox News, December 17, 2012, https://www.youtube.com/watch?v=e_itBjRaR8U.

80. Paul Harvey commentary, *If I Were the Devil,* ABC Radio, April 3, 1965, http://stg.do/9LDc.

81. S.815—Employment Non-Discrimination Act of 2013, 113th Congress (2013–2014), https://www.congress.gov/bill/113th-congress/senate-bill/815.

82. Jacqueline Klima, "U.S. Military 'Hostile' to Christians under Obama; Morale, Retention Devastated," *Washington Times,* April 15, 2015, http://www.washingtontimes.com/news/2015/apr/15/us-military-losing-christians-because-of-hostile-c/?page=all.

83. Austin Ruse, "Naval Chaplain Files Formal Complaint over Christian Persecution," *Breitbart,* June 11, 2015, http://www.breitbart.com/big-government/2015/06/11/naval-chaplain-files-formal-complaint-over-christian-persecution/.

84. "Tolerating Radical Islam but Not Christian Bakers," *Patriot Post,* February 20, 2015, http://patriotpost.us/articles/33326.

85. Adolf Hitler, *Mein Kampf,* the Big Lie, p. 134, as listed on https://www.jewishvirtuallibrary.org/jsource/Holocaust/kampf.html#2.

86. "Freedom, Liberty and Rights," *Samuel Adams Heritage Society,* http://www.samuel-adams-heritage.com/quotes/freedom-liberty.html.

87. C. S. Lewis, *God in the Dock: Essays on Theology and Ethics,* as listed on http://www.goodreads.com/quotes/526469-of-all-tyrannies-a-tyranny-sincerely-exercised-for-the-good.

88. Gerald F. Seib, "In Crisis, Opportunity for Obama," *Wall Street Journal,* updated Nov. 21, 2008, http://www.wsj.com/articles/SB122721278056345271.

89. False flag, *Wikipedia,* https://en.wikipedia.org/wiki/False_flag.

90. Gleiwitz incident, *Wikipedia,* https://en.wikipedia.org/wiki/Gleiwitz_incident.

91. John Hayward, "Carson at CPAC: How to destroy America in 4 steps," *Human Events,* Sunday Mar 17, 2013, http://humanevents.com/2013/03/17/dr-ben-carson-at-cpac-2013-how-to-destroy-america-in-four-easy-steps/.

92. Useful idiot, *Wikipedia,* https://en.wikipedia.org/wiki/Useful_idiot.

93. Todd Starnes, "Pentagon: Religious Proselytizing Is Not Permitted," Fox News Radio, http://radio.foxnews.com/toddstarnes/top-stories/pentagon-religious-proselytizing-is-not-permitted.html.

94. Interview with Neil Clark Warren, "Neil Clark Warren on Finding eHarmony," *NPR,* updated August 17, 2005, published August 17, 2005, http://www.npr.org/templates/story/story.php?storyId=4803877. http://www.npr.org/player/v2/mediaPlayer.html?action=1&t=1&islist=false&id=4803877&m=4803878.

95. Nisha Satkunarajah, "8-year lawsuit settled over US lesbians denied IVF," *BioNews*, October 5, 2009, http://www.bionews.org.uk/page_49295.asp.

96. Ryan T. Anderson, "Government to Ordained Ministers: Celebrate Same-Sex Wedding or Go to Jail," *Daily Signal,* October 18, 2014, http://dailysignal.com/2014/10/18/government-ordained-ministers-celebrate-sex-wedding-go-jail/?utm_source=facebook&utm_medium=social.

97. David Green, "Column: Christian Companies Can't Bow to Sinful Mandate," quote from Hobby Lobby letter, *USA Today,* September 12, 2012, http://usatoday30.usatoday.com/news/opinion/forum/story/2012-09-12/hhs-mandate-birth-control-sue-hobby-lobby/57759226/1.

98. K. Allan Blume, , "'Guilty as Charged,' Cathy Says of Chick-fil-A's Stand on Biblical & Family Values," *Baptist Press*, July 16, 2012, http://www.bpnews.net/38271.

99. *Dhimmitude,* "Dhimmitude: History: Dhimmitude," Rules of dhimmitude, dhimmitude.org, http://www.dhimmitude.org/d_history_dhimmitude.html.

100. "The Global Religious Landscape," *Pew Research Center,* December 18, 2012 http://www.pewforum.org/2012/12/18/global-religious-landscape-exec/.

101. "What Is Scientology?," *Scientology*, http://www.scientology.org/what-is-scientology.html.

102. Cleon Skousen, *The Naked Communist*, Kindle Edition, ASIN: B00B76J804, http://www.amazon.com/Naked-Communist-Book-ebook/dp/B00B76J804/ref=tmm_kin_swatch_0?_encoding=UTF8&qid=&sr=.

103. Jean-Louis Panné, Andrzej Paczkowski, Karel Bartosek, and Aldous Huxley, *The Black Book of Communism,* edited by Stéphane

Courtois, Kindle Edition, ASIN: B017QFW73Y, http://www.amazon.com/Black-Book-Communism-Crimes-Repression-ebook/dp/B017QFW73Y/ref=mt_kindle?_encoding=UTF8&me=.

104. Curtis Bowers (writer/director), *Agenda: Grinding America Down,* Copybook Heading Productions LLC, listed at http://www.imdb.com/title/tt2360880/, https://vimeo.com/ondemand/agendagrindingamerica/63749370.

105. Michael Swift, *Homosexual Manifesto,* reprinted from *The Congressional Record of the United States Congress*; first printed in *Gay Community News*, February 15–21, 1987; http://www.massresistance.org/docs/gen/09b/Redeeming_rainbow/chapters/Chapter-13.pdf.

106. Marshall Kirk and Erastes Pill, *The Overhauling of Straight America,* http://www.massresistance.org/docs/gen/09b/Redeeming_rainbow/chapters/Chapter-13.pdf.

107. by London_gay, "The list of Gay Themed TV Series on IMDb," created September 23 2012, updated October 10, 2013, http://www.imdb.com/list/ls008977817/.

108. List of animated television programs with LGBT characters, *Wikipedia,* https://en.wikipedia.org/wiki/List_of_animated_television_programs_with_LGBT_characters.

109. Ray Comfort, *Evolution vs. God*: *Shaking the Foundations of Faith*, 2013, http://www.evolutionvsgod.com/.

110. Mark Bennett, "Defining Reasonable Doubt," *bennettandbennett.com*, July 30, 2007, http://blog.bennettandbennett.com/2007/07/defining-reasonable-doubt/.

111. Richard Stengel, "Cover Story: One Document, Under Siege," *Time,* June 23, 2011, http://content.time.com/time/nation/article/0,8599,2079445,00.html.

112. Curtis Kalin, "CNN Anchor: 'Our Rights Do Not Come from God,'" *CNS News*, February 12, 2015, http://www.cnsnews.com/blog/curtis-kalin/cnn-anchor-our-rights-do-not-come-god.

113. Gene Roddenberry and Jerome Bixby, *Star Trek,* "The Day of the Dove," season 3, episode 7, 1968, listed at http://www.imdb.com/title/tt0708427/.

www.ingramcontent.com/pod-product-compliance
Lightning Source LLC
Chambersburg PA
CBHW060924040426
42445CB00011B/787

9780692615584